CEDRIC NOT THE ENTERTAINER

"A LIFE'S JOURNEY AND THEN SOME"

Cedric M. Cason

ISBN: 979-8-89212-835-3

Dedication

I dedicate this book to my mother, Gloria Anderson, and my stepfather, Eddie G. Anderson Jr. I also would like to dedicate this book to my beautiful wife, Rachel Wairimu Mwanu-
Cason.

I have been a best man in five weddings, out of which only two are still successful: George and Gina, who married in 1982 (40+ years), and Tony and Steph, who married in 1995 (23+ years). I would say both of these couples were equally yoked because their foundation was steadfast and secure with God.

It took a while for God to prepare me before I met you, "But God." His timing is always perfect. We have been married for 29 years, and I feel like we are just beginning. I love you; I cherish you, and without you, there would be no me.

Acknowledgment

I told my wife years ago; I was going to write an autobiography. Therefore, I would like to thank my wife for reminding me that when I say I am going to do something, I always do it. I also would like to thank our lead Pastor, Bishop Sykes, for telling people in his messages to do what GOD has put on your minds and always finish what you start. I would also like to thank my cousins, James Earl Jones and Dorothy Wofford Witherspoon, for their books that gave me insight into our ancestors.

Contents

About the Author

Cedric Cason, new in the writing world, has decided to share his life's journey from living in poverty-stricken projects, being raised by a single mother, and discovering a father's value as a teenager. From fleeing the drug scene and a bounty on his head in E. St. Louis to joining the United States Marine Corps and getting betrayed, he shares the destruction of his career and family, which led him to brew suicidal thoughts. When all he could do was breathe, he exhaled and found success in the private sector as well as in the boardroom.

He has been married to his beautiful wife, Rachel Mwana-Cason, from Nairobi, Kenya, for over 29 years. Together, they raised their son, Isaac Cason, who is now an 18-year-old college student. It's a journey only Cedric can explain and share the lows and highs that made him who he is today. Get ready for a roller coaster ride through Cedric's life.

Foreword

By Erinn Cooper

In this day and age of ambiguity and watered-down versions of everything from news to relationships, I consider this book to be a breath of fresh air that will bring all who read it back to reality. A reality where one has to work hard and pray harder because the world wants to devour all that we are or will ever be. In this book, Brother Cedric steps from being a hustler, to a Marine, husband, father, friend, and man of God. Ced is not afraid to show us how low one can go and how God is still willing to love us, be there to pick us up out of the dirt, dust us off, and use us!

This book is raw, relative, and relatable. If it does not teach us to grow in emotional intelligence and spiritual maturity, then we need to read it twice.

Glory to God!

Gunnery Sergeant / Pastor Erinn Cooper

Preface

This book has been in the making all my life. Why now, only GOD knows. The first chapter is to honor my ancestors, and the rest of the book is a detailed story about my childhood, teenage years, and adult life. I have hurt people, and I have been hurt by people, and in this book, I ask for forgiveness, and I have forgiven all. This book is one of the most difficult accomplishments of my life. It was also therapeutic for me.

Chapter 1: My Family/My Lineage
(From the Slave Ships to Mississippi/Arkansas to East St. Louis)

The social evil of slavery strengthened its roots in America in the early 1600s when Africans were kidnapped by Portuguese soldiers and brought to the British Colonies of Virginia. They were then exploited by English Colonists for their political and personal interests. This practice shaped the concept of enslaving African people, regardless of age and gender; men, women, or children, no one was safe from this barbaric practice. The practice continued for centuries, and it wasn't until the Civil Rights Movement was at its utmost rise in the mid-19th century that Black people found a practical implication of their legal rights, mainly credited to the 13th and 14th Amendments. These rights were made a part of the constitution and previously obtained under the presidency of Abraham Lincoln. However, despite being granted legal rights, Black Americans still faced major discrimination and were often treated differently by the White supremacists, which started another Civil Rights Movement in 1954.

It was a prolonged battle against undeniable injustice and brutality from the early 1600s till the late 1800s. During this time, black people were forcefully captured across Africa, enslaved, and forced to work mainly on the tobacco, rice, and indigo plantations. They were brought on massive slave ships and held captive in confined spaces. Due to the lack of ventilation and lavatory services, all sorts of contagious diseases spread across these ships among the enslaved people and crew members. The enslaved Black people also faced the atrocities of brutal torture from the crew members upon trivial matters, and more so when they tried to commit suicide.

Unable to bear the horrid conditions aboard the slave ships and terrified of the future that awaited them, many enslaved people tried to commit suicide by jumping off the ship. However, their desperate attempts to escape a life of slavery often failed because of the fish nets tied around the entire ship, specifically put there to catch the enslaved people who would throw themselves in the sea. Despite all that, due to various fatal illnesses, most people, whether they were crew members or poor enslaved people, who sailed in those ships never reached their destination.

After getting ashore, the enslaved Black people who somehow managed to survive were sold off in markets like animals where all sorts of people would buy them and use them for their needs, mainly as farmers on fields. Black lives were treated more like property than actual human lives, as they were used and abused in all forms.

Throughout the Atlantic Slave Trade, over 12.05 million Africans were enslaved and loaded onto ships. However, only around only 10 million of them actually reached American soil. On the other hand, around one-third of the population of the African continent was wiped out due to the slave trade. The Atlantic Slave Trade is an example of what human greed for money and power can do and how many innocent lives are ruined in the process.

Out of these millions - not hundreds, not thousands, but millions - of enslaved Africans were also my great-great-grandparents, both maternal and paternal. They were shipped to America as enslaved people, where they met and fell in love with one another and started a family before ultimately being freed around 1860.

The lineage from my father's side of the family includes my great-great-grandmother, Mandy, who was also enslaved. She was sold to a family named Whitecross as a little girl. She had four children named Joe, Tom, Mary, and Ben. Mandy and her children were then sold to the Wofford's in Meridian, Mississippi. All her children grew up there. Tom and Joe would later go on to settle in different parts of Arkansas.

My great-grandfather, Joe Wofford, served as a Revolutionary War soldier and was an active member of the Whig party, supporting independence for the Colonies.

Joe later met and married my great-grandmother, Callie. They had five children together: Jerry, Cathea, my grandfather Dennis, Wrethard, and another girl who unfortunately died as a baby. Callie also passed away, and Joe remarried Roberta Brinker, with whom he went on to have 12 children. The family relocated to Arkansas when my grandfather was around ten years old.

In Arkansas, my grandfather, Dennis, married my grandmother, Lugenia Guyton, daughter of Joe and Mary Lamar Guyton, in 1919. My Grandparents, Dennis and Lugenia, were blessed with nine children: Joseph, Lebertha, John, Bernice, my father Leodis (Leo), Catherine, James, Wilbur, and Maxine.

My biological father, Leodis Wofford

The lineage on my mother's side included my great-great-grandfather, Brice Connolly, who was kidnapped in Africa along with his two brothers, Ban Butler and Tom

Evans. Only the Lord knows the amount of terror and hardship the brothers endured on their long journey to a North Carolina port. When they arrived in North Carolina between 1820 and 1835, they were sold to different masters.

No one, including me, can imagine how their souls must have shattered as they were separated from their homeland and family and were enslaved on slave ships. Then, as if the world had not been cruel enough to them, they were also torn apart from the only familiar faces of one another in an entirely new country, as they were bought by not only different but also strange people.

My great-great-grandfather, Brice, was bought by a master in Mississippi. As an enslaved person, he was forced to work on a cotton plantation; that was how he spent the next 40 years of his life. Although enslaved people faced endless hardships and miseries, love prevailed when he and my great-great-grandmother, Parthenia Connolly, met each other.

My great-great-grandmother, Parthenia, was an Irish Bond slave from Ireland. Apart from being beautiful, she was also smart. Back in those days, reading and writing were not the skills usually taught to enslaved people, but she could do all that. She was also a kind person as she taught Brice how to read and write as well.

After the Civil War ended, my great-great-grandparents were both freed, after which they got married. Upon being freed from the chains of slavery that had bound him for over 40 years, Brice did not want any reminders of that time, and he did not want to take his master's name. That is when Parthenia came up with an idea. She suggested that since they knew her last name, Brice could also take the same last name as hers. He agreed, and thus, Connolly became our family name, and my great-great-grandfather became Brice Connolly.

Brice and Parenthia had nine children together, the third one being Wyatt Connolly, my paternal great-grandfather.

As found in our family's history, after the complete abolition of slavery during Reconstruction, my great-grandfather, Wyatt Connolly, bought land of around 300 acres in Arkabutla, Mississippi. On his land, he cultivated his farm and built a house in the center, which he called the "Home House." During this process, he also married Sharlett Jeeter, who was half-African and half-Indian. Together, they had eleven children. One of those eleven children was my grandmother, Mary Connolly, born in June 1899 in Savage, Mississippi.

The lineage on my maternal grandfather's side of the family firstly included my great-grandfather, Samuel Franklin, and my great-grandmother, Harriet Ogletree Franklin-Richard. Together, they had seven children named Josephine F. Henry Hawthorne, Mamie F. Burrows,

Bessie F. Tucker, Ruth Franklin, Hattie F. Waters, and my grandfather, Archie Franklin.

My paternal grandfather, Archie Franklin, and grandmother, Mary Connolly, who later became Mary Franklin, were married on May 12, 1923, in Polk, Arkansas. They had ten children; Leon Franklin (Ruth), Fred Franklin (Everlena), Wyatt Franklin (Myrtle), Morris Franklin (Sarah), Archi Franklin (Frances), Clifton Franklin (Lela), Mary Swanson (Wiley), Ira Lee Franklin (Beatrice), Mildred McGaughy (Willie), and my mother, Gloria Anderson (Eddie).

Whether it was my paternal great-great-grandparents or maternal, they were all taught to read and write while they were still enslaved. They were also freed during and after the Civil War. After that, they were able to buy land for themselves. In both cases of my great-great-grandparents, the Connolly's or the Franklin's, their land had belonged to them since the Reconstruction era. The land was plentiful and beautiful, but later on, it was either taken or forced to sell very cheaply.

Coming to my family, my mother, Gloria Franklin, was born on October 12, 1938. She was actually my grandparents' 14th child, who was born after three of my grandparents' children passed away. My mother was born in the Township of Proctor, the City of Edmondson, State of Arkansas.

As for my father, not much of his personal information is known besides his family history. That is because my mother, Gloria Franklin, and Leo Wofford were never together as a couple. On my birth certificate, my father's name was "Legally Omitted," his race was listed as "Negro," and his age was listed as 30 years.

On the other hand, my mother, Gloria Franklin, had three children. The first-born was George Cason, the second-born child was my sister, Anita Franklin (Hobson), and I was her last-born child.

Since my parents never had a proper relationship, my father was not around or a part of our family. Therefore, I was never introduced to or got in touch with him in my early years. My mother received her nursing degree and became a registered nurse in April 1974, all while raising her three children to the best of her abilities.

When I was 5 or maybe 6 years old, I was introduced to my father. Even after that, he only came around now and then.

As I look at my grandparents, Dennis and Lugenia's 50th wedding anniversary picture, taken in 1969, in St. Louis, MO, with the Wofford family, I am nowhere to be found. By that time, I must have been around six years of age, but since I was not present in the family, it shows that my father's family was unaware that my father, Leo, had a son.

Regarding my relationship with my family, my siblings, George and Anita, and I had a close relationship while growing up. We grew up in a very low-income family, raised by a single mother until I was 13 years old and my siblings were even older. My sibling and I bond because we survived living in a poverty project home, looking out for each other.

I also shared a great relationship with my aunts and uncles – my mother's siblings. My mother had seven brothers. Unfortunately, the eighth one, Uncle Wyatt, passed away before I was born. My Uncle Fred and Uncle Morris lived in Chicago and Detroit, respectively. So, since my uncles Leon, Archie (Bud), Cliff, Wiley, and Ira (Boots) lived nearby, I always looked up to them, and they played an important role in my life growing up – they were like father figures in my developing years since my real father wasn't around.

My uncles were known for being hardworking. They owned companies in different industries, for example, construction, hogs, and pigs. According to my knowledge, most of my uncles who moved to Centreville also worked at a company named J.J. Brouk & Company in St. Louis before moving on to industries like Monsanto around East St. Louis. My uncles were all also very handsome and were known as the "Franklin Brothers," except for my Uncle Wiley, whose last name was Swanson.

My uncles Cliff, Wily, and Boots had many children, and so I had a lot of cousins to play with growing up. Of course, being the youngest cousin also had its perks; I was spoiled not only by the elders but also by my older cousins.

If I think about my family history, it is very rich and diverse. Despite experiencing things that we can only imagine, my ancestors survived through whatever life threw their way, and here I am today, a result of their perseverance.

My Ancestry DNA

Ethnicity Estimate ↗

● Nigeria	23% ›
● Cameroon, Congo & Western Bantu Peoples	18% ›
● England & Northwestern Europe	16% ›
● Mali	8% ›
● Ivory Coast & Ghana	8% ›
● Jewish	6% ›
● Wales	6% ›
● Benin & Togo	5% ›
● Scotland	5% ›
● Senegal	2% ›
● Southern Bantu Peoples	1% ›
● Basque	1% ›

My great grandparents, Wyatt and Sharlett Jetter Connolly, with my grandmother, Mary Connolly (the little girl on the far left).

Dennis and Lugenia's 50th wedding anniversary. My father is wearing the black tux and bowtie.

Dennis & Lugenia's 50th Wedding Anniversary Celebration, 1969, St. Louis, Mo.

Chapter 2: Fire Station Centreville, Il
(My life during the height of the Civil Rights Movement)

Have you ever noticed the happiness that resides in children? Free from all worldly responsibilities and worries, children are unaware of the harsh and cruel realities of this world. With their protected innocence, they roam freely with zero burdens on their shoulders, proving that their naivety is indeed a blessing in disguise.

Like most children, I was also a happy-go-lucky kid. Looking back at my childhood, one could easily tell that I was living in my fantasy world. I was born and raised in Centreville, the poorest city in the state of Illinois, as well as one of the poorest cities in the United States. To give you a better idea of the economic status of the neighborhood, the median income is still around $17,441 per household. However, despite growing up in an area like that, I cannot recall a single incident or event that caused me any sadness, ever. Because that is the way kids usually are; living in their dreamland, far away from the deep despair.

The city of Centreville was located just East of St. Louis, on a Mississippi River floodplain; it was also known as the American Bottom. Because of its location, it often experienced flooding and raw sewage disposal problems because of the area's inefficient and inadequate drainage system. Then, on May 6, 2021, the city ceased to exist after it was incorporated into the new city of Cahokia Heights.

I may have been born in a poor neighborhood, but I lived a happy childhood. My mother, siblings, and I lived in my grandparents, Big Mama and Big Daddy's house. My grandparents had built this house from the ground up when they migrated from the South, from Mississippi, to be exact, and moved to E. St. Louis in 1947. The reason they moved to E. St. Louis was that their third oldest son, Wyatt "Snoot" Franklin, was murdered by his wife in Aberdeen, and Big Mama became traumatized by the incident. She had quite a difficult time living in Aberdeen after that because everything reminded her of her son. Two of Big Daddy's siblings, Aunt Josie and Uncle Samuel, lived up North in E. St. Louis. Despite E. St. Louis being known for having one of the worst riots in US history back in 1917, Big Daddy thought it was the best place to go since his siblings were also there. And so, the entire family moved right next to Aunt Josie's house; that is when my grandparents built the house where I spent my childhood. I will never forget that house because that is the place where I lived until I was seven years old and made countless unforgettable memories.

As I have mentioned before, I was the youngest of three siblings, so I had an older brother, George, and a sister, Anita. The three of us did not have the same fathers, but that never impacted our relationship because we loved and cared for each other regardless. For my mother, however, it must have been a different story. Being a single mother with three back in the 1960s, one could barely imagine the stress that came with that situation. On top of that, the financial burden of not only supporting herself but also her three children must have been too much for my mother to cope with. I believe that was the reason we lived in my grandparents' house, because my mother could not afford a home on her own.

While I have heard great things about Big Mama and Big Daddy, unfortunately, I did not get to spend much time with them. I never met my grandmother, Mary Franklin, as she passed away five months before I was born. I did hear all kinds of stories about her as a child. Stories such as how Big Mama used to make red wine from the grapes she grew in the backyard and how she would make it in a 3 ft tall ceramic container with a lid.

Growing up, I also heard the infamous story of how gracefully my grandmother had passed away without anybody having a clue. So the story goes that Big Mama was sitting on the front porch of our house one day when she asked one of my uncles to dash to the store to buy her a beer. And while my uncle was out for the chore, my mother noticed that Big Mama was resting peacefully in her rocking chair. She paid no mind to it and went about her day. However, when my uncle returned with the beer, the family realized that she had passed away. It was later discovered that she had suffered a massive heart attack. My grandmother died a very silent death, but I believe that seeing her resting peacefully in her rocking chair brought the family some comfort that maybe she did not feel a lot of pain and her departure from this world had been seamless.

On the other hand, while I did meet my grandfather, my memories of him are so vague that I can barely recall them as I was only 2 years and a few months old when he also passed away. I heard all kinds of stories about my grandfather growing up as well, especially about how much he loved me. According to my mother, Big Daddy used to spend a lot of time with me, bouncing me up and down on his knee.

Even after Big Daddy passed away, we continued living in my grandparents' house for the next five years until we had no choice but to leave.

When it came to our house, it was the largest house on 3rd Avenue. The address was 4242 3rd Avenue, Centreville, Il. There were cherry trees, pecan, walnut trees, purple and yellow plums, and red and yellow grapes on the property. There were also many apple trees, and I remember apple trees lining the block. Even though the house had an indoor bathroom, there was also an out-house on the property.

When I say that my whole world revolved around that block, I truly mean it. I had the freedom to roam around that block as I wished. I could go anywhere and to anyone's house as long as it was on the same block. Since most of my aunts and uncles also lived on 3rd Avenue, I was fortunate to have been surrounded by family growing up.

My mother, being the youngest of 10 children, meant that I could hardly keep count of how many cousins I had. I am in no way complaining, however, as it made for a very fun-filled childhood, being surrounded by children of all ages. Everywhere I went, no matter whose house I was in, I felt at home. Being one of the youngest children in the family, everyone looked out for me, and I used to look up to all my siblings and cousins and follow them wherever they went.

My relatives owned the majority of the houses on 3rd Avenue, and my Aunt Mary, my mother's oldest sister, lived across the street from us. As a child, I enjoyed spending time with her because she always treated me to sweet things like candy. I remember one incident in particular that stuck with me throughout my childhood. One day, I was in the kitchen with Aunt Mary, watching her make some Kool-Aid. As she was doing that, I did not see her putting the Kool-Aid powder in the pitcher. The only thing I saw was her picking up the empty pitcher and walking it over to the sink to fill it with water. So, when I saw the clear pitcher filling up with cherry Kool-Aid, I genuinely thought that my Aunt Mary had the only faucet in the neighborhood, if not the whole world, that poured out instant Kool-Aid. After that, I must have tried to get Kool-Aid out of that faucet for at least a year until I decided to give up.

Although I had a good relationship with all my uncles, I was perhaps the closest to my Uncle Bud, who lived a few houses down the street from us. Uncle Bud was the father figure in my life whom I looked up to the most. Whenever I knocked at his door or found him in his workshop, he always greeted me with a big smile. Then, he would hand me a quarter. A quarter may not seem like much these days, but back in the day, a quarter could get you a lot of candy and soda. However, before the quarter came out, Uncle Bud always tried to teach me about building or fixing something. There were even times when I would try to return his quarter to him to let him know that I simply wanted to hang out with him. Of course, he never took it back.

Not once in my life did Uncle Bud ever tell me, "Go on, get out of here." As a matter of fact, I cannot remember being told by any of my uncles or aunties to leave. No matter whose house I visited, I was treated like I was part of the household. I always ate what was being served, whether it was breakfast, lunch, or dinner.

I have many great and some crazy memories of living on 3rd Avenue. When learning how to ride a bike, I remember I had to put my legs through the frame because I was too small to sit on the seat. I used to follow one of

Aunt Mary's sons, Harold, wherever he went. I also used to ride on the handlebars of his bike. One time, I recall my foot getting caught in the spikes of the front wheel and flipping over head first with Harold flying over me. I thought that I had broken my foot, and Harold thought the same, which is why he carried me all the way home. Fortunately, that was not the case.

Another time, while hanging out with Harold, I was sitting on his handlebars riding down the street when this big dog came out of nowhere and started barking at us. Harold tried to speed up, but the dog caught up with us and bit me on the leg. So, Harold did the only logical thing he could think of; he stopped the bike and kicked the dog in the nose, making it run away. Again, he had to take me home, this time with a bleeding leg from a dog bite.

Then there was this one time when I was playing with my siblings outside our house when we came across a bee nest. One of us must have hit the nest because the next thing I remember was getting stung multiple times all over my body and face.

Another memorable thing about living on 3rd Avenue was the local fire station, which was around a block and a half away, where I had a lot of fun times. The most interesting thing about it was that it served as my kindergarten classroom. My classmates and I used to sit next to the fire trucks during kindergarten, and whenever the bell rang, we had to rush from our tables and chairs and stand against the wall until the fire trucks left.

Some of my older cousins were volunteer firemen, and I loved seeing them jump into action and take off to fight a fire. Every time they left, I got into trouble for running outside to see where the smoke was so I could know where they were headed.

As I was used to chasing after the trucks, one incident, in particular, has stayed with me to this day. One early morning on the weekend, while out playing in the street, I heard the fire station bell ringing, and out of nowhere, I saw three of my cousins running toward the fire station. Without giving it a thought, I ran behind them and actually made it to the station just as they were taking off. As I was watching them, one of my cousins saw me standing right outside the fire station door and screamed at the top of his lungs, "Stop!" He jumped out of the fire truck and yelled, "Cedric! How did you get here?" But before I could say anything, he grabbed me by the back of my pants and hurled me up in the air until I landed on the back of the fire truck on top of the hoses.

So there I was, on top of the fire truck, holding on for dear life, watching the smoke get closer as the fire truck sped toward the burning house with its siren blasting, waking up the entire neighborhood in the process. The entire time, I kept on thinking, "This is the best day of my life," as we got nearer to the burning house that was only about four blocks away. When the truck came to an abrupt stop, I rushed to climb down, thinking I could assist in fighting the fire, which lasted only two seconds before it was put out. Suddenly, another cousin grabbed me from behind, asking at the same time, "How did you get on the truck?" while taking me toward the rest of the onlookers. I didn't really understand the gravity of the situation then; all I cared about was that I had just had the best ride of my life.

During my early childhood, the Civil Rights Movement was at its peak. However, I was too young to understand what that was all about. Although I can now appreciate what the men and women were fighting for and how that has undoubtedly influenced not just my life but the lives of millions of people in the United States, I was just a kid back then. I was too busy enjoying the freedom that living on 3rd Avenue granted me.

As they say, all good things come to an end, and that is what happened to me. My entire world came crashing down when, one day, my brother, sister, and I were playing with candles and fire. My brother George was lighting the curtains on fire and then blowing them out, which we thought was harmless. However, one time, the flame grew so quickly that we could not put out the fire, and it started to spread. Before we knew it, the whole house was filled with smoke. We somehow managed to put it out with help from our neighboring family members, but it's safe to say that the real hell broke loose when my mother got home, and we all got a good whipping for our mischief.

On a later date, I found out that one of my uncles and his wife, who lived just behind our house, had lost their first two children in a house fire. So, it was understandable why my mother was so furious when she found out that we had almost burned down our home.

Soon afterward, we had to move out of our grandparents' house. It was falling apart and was no longer safe to live in. Luckily, around that time in 1968, President Johnson signed the Civil Rights Act of 1968, also known as the Fair Housing Act, providing equal housing opportunities regardless of race, religion, or national origin. That same year, we moved into the brand-new two-bedroom, one-bath projects.

Living in my grandparents' house on 3rd Avenue were some of the best years of my life. I made countless memories there, which I will cherish forever, but as we decided to move from my childhood home, I also looked forward to what more life had in store for me.

Chapter 3: Life in the Projects

After having no choice but to leave my grandparents' house on 3rd Avenue, my family and I moved into our new home in the projects. The address was 6703 Clarita, Centreville, Illinois, and we lived here from 1968 to 1973 until my mom could make enough money to move us to a better location.

I lived in the projects from the first grade through sixth grade, and I have a lot of memories from that time; some very exciting, others, not so much.

As I have mentioned before, I was a happy-go-lucky kid, just like any other normal child my age. However, there was something different about me that I was unable to comprehend at the time. Now that I am older and more aware, I can tell what it was, but back then, neither I nor the adults around me could figure out what was wrong with me, and so I was labeled a troublemaker for my antics.

Back when I was in grade school, it was very difficult for me to stay still or seated all the time. It was hard for me to maintain focus or remain attentive during class. I was quite hyperactive and impulsive and used to bounce off the walls. Since I could not pay attention to something for too long, I always had multiple things going on that kept me engaged. For instance, I would keep moving or fidgeting with something in my hands. My mind would also be occupied by a million thoughts, all just circling around in my head at the same time. It was like a motor was constantly running in my head that would never shut off.

All of these things that I used to do made it seem like I was not paying attention in class, even though I was. My grades were proof of that, but during class, my actions mattered more than my grades, so I often found myself in trouble with my teachers.

Back then, I did not know what was wrong with me, just that I was different from the other kids. However, now that my son has been diagnosed with ADHD, I have come to realize that the issues I used to have and the way I behaved were because I had ADHD, too; the only difference is that I never got diagnosed with it. For those who may not know, ADHD stands for Attention Deficit Hyperactivity Disorder and is a neurodevelopmental disorder that most commonly entails trouble focusing, being overly active, and being compulsive – basically everything that I was dealing with.

I have had ADHD my entire life and learned to manage it better as I grew older, but as a kid, I was not as self-disciplined. I had organization issues, and I always struggled when it came to prioritizing my projects and assignments.

Because of my ADHD problems, my teachers eventually grew sick and tired of me. I could never stay put in my seat; I was either bouncing in my chair, bouncing off the walls, or I would randomly get up from my seat and roam in the classroom, and all of this used to happen in the middle of class.

My teachers were literally fed up with me, and because I hadn't been diagnosed, they thought all of these things I was doing were deliberate and were part of my mischief, while the reality was completely the opposite. My behavior was something I could not control, but I still got punished for it. I remember receiving a lot of corporal punishment in grade school, especially when I was in my first, second, and third grades. I recall being paddled and being hit on the inside of my wrist with a ruler. Once the ruler slapping started, it became a usual trend. Every other teacher would come, get annoyed by my constant movements, and would end up hitting me on my palms.

I remember once, when I was in third grade, one of the teachers hit me so hard and so many times that my wrist started bleeding. Going back home that day, I showed it to my mom, who was understandably furious. The very next day, my mom came to school to have a word with the teacher who had hit me and the school administration. Needless to say, the physical punishment, or, to be more accurate, the "physical torture" stopped after that.

Although the days of being hit in class were behind me, the mental punishment never ended. I would often be scolded and singled out in class for my behavior. You would assume that because I still maintained good grades, the teachers would cut me some slack, but that was not the case. In fact, I remember my third-grade teacher tried their best to hold me back a year. All because of my behavior.

When my mom got wind of her scheme, she once again barged into the teacher's lounge, from where she was taken to the administration office to have a proper discussion. My teachers had no solid justification for holding me back a year. Eventually, I moved up to the fourth grade with my classmates.

Because of my helpless condition, I was bullied a lot since the first grade; however, by the time I reached the third grade, I had had enough, which is when I fought back and, in turn, became a bully myself. Cedric Johnson was one of the bullies I had been dealing with since grade one. However, little did I know that he was about to become my best friend.

I hated bullying; however, in order to protect myself, I befriended Cedric and started hanging out with him and the other bullies, which also made me one of them. So, technically, I had become a bully to protect myself from becoming a victim. Once I became a part of the 'bully group' and got close to Cedric, I learned a valuable piece of information: bullies would only bully you if you let them do it.

Cedric and I were always competitive, which is also why we challenged each other from time to time. But in a way, we fed off of each other and would get in a lot of trouble together.

Cedric and I were very mischievous and usually up to no good. I remember that we were once playing with fire in the old wheat field that was next to the projects. Cedric and I accidentally set the field on fire. We did try to put it out, but there was only so much two young boys could do on their own against the growing flames. When we realized we could not control it or put it out ourselves, we just fled the scene back to our project apartments and acted like we had no clue about the fire.

With practically the whole field up in flames, people from the projects called the fire department. I remember standing outside the apartment with all the other residents, observing the fire from afar and acting just as surprised as everyone else. The fire was eventually put out, and just as the crowd of people was about to disperse, a voice from the crowd got everyone's attention,

"It was Cedric Cason and Cedric Johnson that started the fire because I saw them running away from the fields when the fire started."

During the walk back to the apartment, my sister, who was also there, kept threatening me that she would tell my mom what happened the moment she got back. What happened when she did is quite obvious; I was severely punished for the whole fiasco at the wheat field.

Cedric and I always got into trouble together; however, none of the punishments ever came in between our friendship. After every punishment, we would just go back to each other, share how we were punished, and would end up doing something similar again.

When Cedric and I entered the fifth grade, we started skipping school. We would get on the city bus and ride around the projects. One day, the bus driver, an old white man, asked if we would like to ride to downtown St. Louis. We both looked at each other and simultaneously said yes, which is how it all started, and we started skipping school frequently after that. We would get on the bus, get off in downtown St. Louis, where we would wonder and roam around, and then after a few hours, we would wait for the same bus driver to come and drop us back at the projects.

Since I had been hanging out with Cedric for over two years at that point, I had also gotten pretty great at making excuses. So, the day before we started skipping school, I told my homeroom teacher, Mr. Green, that I had a dental appointment and wouldn't be able to make it to class the next day. Well, that dental appointment lasted a good week and may have gone on for a lot longer had I not been busted.

Everything was going smoothly; Cedric and I skipped school every day and spent that time roaming around downtown St. Louis. But our time to get caught was nearing. As the week came to an end, Cedric and I were getting ready to get on the city bus and ride to downtown

St. Louis. However, when I got on and looked around, my eyes met with my sister Anita's, whose mouth was agape, staring at me in disbelief. The jig was up.

As soon as my mom came home, Anita, ever the tattletale, told her that she had seen me riding on the city bus during the school timings. When confronted, I had to come clean and eventually ended up telling my mother everything.

As expected, my mother was furious and took me to school the next day. She told Mr. Green everything. Mr. Green was quite upset and disappointed in me. I was grounded as a result and for a very long time.

Cedric, on the other hand, continued. He skipped school that day, too, and only I knew the actual reason why he had not shown up at school. When Cedric did return to school, he was not the same as before. Something had happened to him on the bus, and I never saw the old Cedric Johnson again after that day. He became very distant and quiet and stopped socializing with anyone. As I grew older, things started to make sense as I started thinking, why would an old man ask two young boys to ride his bus for free, and that too not once but multiple times? I still do not know what exactly happened, but one thing that I know for sure is that Cedric never got on that bus again. Later on in life, I found out that Cedric died as an adult due to complications from AIDS.

***

Life in the projects was more of a hustling one. Most of the families that lived in the projects consisted of single mothers trying to raise their children in the best way they could. Most of the kids living in the projects were out of control; there used to be a lot of fights and a lot of trash-talking about who had the fattest mom or who was the poorest, or who wore the ugliest clothes. We were all hardly making ends meet, but people always looked for someone who was even below them. That was their way of feeling better about themselves and their circumstances.

It was mostly just me and my older siblings, George and Anita, who stayed away from all kinds of fights and trash talks. Both my siblings were introverts but also very intelligent. They were always busy doing their homework or reading books. I was the complete opposite of the two — an extrovert who was always hanging outside with other kids in the projects and, as usual, getting in trouble. I was out all the time playing games like kissing a girl, catching a girl, and all such misbehaving feats that wouldn't fly today.

Like the other mothers, my mom also tried her best to provide the best life she could for her kids. Back in 1970, I remember my mom took us to see the live concert of Jackson 5 in downtown St. Louis. It was my first-ever concert, and I fell in love with music after I saw Michael Jackson and his brothers performing live. I was awestruck by not just the performance but the overall vibes at the concert. When I came back to the projects, I was thrown down from cloud nine, but I would never be able to forget my first-ever live concert.

Around the time when I was in sixth grade, my mom had graduated from nursing school and was making decent money, because of which she was able to buy a house of her own. I remember being super happy and super excited as I knew that we could finally move out of the projects.

Life in the projects wasn't easy; however, for me, it was full of adventures. My siblings and my mother tried their best to keep me reigned. However, my ADHD was something that never let me stay in control. Even now, there are a lot of things that are not in my control, but as an adult, I am more organized, self-disciplined, and know how to set my priorities.

Me in grade school

Me in the third grade

Chapter 4: Elmijah Homes

I was so happy once we had moved out of the projects. Our new home was in a housing project called the Elmijah Homes, located at 702 West Avenue, Centreville, IL.

As soon as I entered the house, I began to look around and check every corner. I was really curious. It was a single-family home with three bedrooms, two upstairs and the master bedroom downstairs. Oh, boy! This house was bigger and better than the previous one. Finally, me and my brother had our own room, and we didn't have to share it with our sister anymore. We all were growing up and couldn't stay in one room forever. Having a space to ourselves was a relief.

Another thing I liked about this house was the backyard and garage. We had our own garage and a backyard with a cherry tree. Times had changed, and I was slowly forgetting about the life we had in the projects.

It was summertime when I and one of my close friends named Juan Brown, who lived in the same neighborhood, planned to go fishing at the canal on a Saturday morning with his older brothers. As I said earlier, I loved going out, so that Saturday, before she left for work, my mother said to me, "No matter what, you are not allowed to leave this house today."

It might sound threatening but I was used to hearing such warnings from time to time. As usual, I would wait for Mom to leave, then jet out of the house. But this Saturday, my older sister weighed in and stated, "If you leave this house today, I'm going to tell Mom, and you'll be busted!" So, I stayed at home that Saturday and missed the fishing trip with my friend.

Later that afternoon, I received a phone call from my friend Cedric, who was still living in the projects. He told me they had just pulled Juan Brown's body out of the canal because he had drowned to death. My eyes went wide, and I was in utter shock. I did not want to believe it and was very upset. The thought of losing my friend was terrifying. At that point, I had no clue what depression was. For months, I was upset and depressed but didn't know what my feelings were.

One day, I was hanging out with my mother. We were at her favorite place, the beauty salon. Surprisingly, Juan Brown's mom was there too. My mother's head was underneath the blow dryer when Juan's mother began calling me Juan and grabbing me by the arm. My mother had to jump out of her chair and grab me, explaining to Juan's mom that this wasn't her child. I don't think she ever got over the loss of her son. All I remember from that event is that I was confused, and the thought of Juan never left my mind.

Growing up at Elmijah Homes, I was in love with my new neighborhood and was always looking for ways in which I could earn money. I went against the wishes of my siblings and took a paper route in our new neighborhood. I became the local paper boy for all families living in the area. It was just a one-block radius with about a total of sixty single-family homes. My route covered West Ave, Sterling St., and Nelson Ave.

I loved being the paperboy because I noticed how most families waited for me to come and toss them the paper. It kind of motivated me because I felt valued. The rainy days were the longest because I had to individually wrap each paper into plastic sheets so they would not get wet. Sometimes, my older brother would give me a hand.

The toughest part of being a paperboy was collection day. All of a sudden, no one was home. I rang doorbells and knocked on doors, but there was no answer. After a week, I would just stop delivering papers, and then all of a sudden, they would appear, waving at me and calling out when they saw me on the street.

I would always say the same thing: "My boss told me I can't deliver the paper here anymore until the account is current." Lo and behold, they would suddenly pay the bill. One day, I was knocking at this door on Sterling Street, and I was about to walk away when someone finally opened the door. I turned around and was astonished to see who it was.

It was one of my uncles standing there in a bathrobe. My jaw dropped when I saw my uncle.

"What are you doing here?" he said and looked me up and down. I told him I was working as a paper boy. We exchanged a few words, and he asked me what the total bill was. I was not expecting anything from him, but damn! He paid the bill and tipped me as well. It was the biggest tip I have ever got in my life. All my uncles have passed, but I still will never tell who it was.

After getting comfortable in the new neighborhood and recovering from the loss of Juan Brown, I met up with a couple of other friends, like Brian Frierson, Andrew Gilmore, and Ricky Thompson. We used to hang out a lot when I was in junior high.

Brian lived about a mile away, and Andrew lived across the street from us in the apartment area. When we got bored, we used to do silly things to keep ourselves entertained. Brian had a big family with older sisters, and I believe Dre was an only child.

One day, Brian, Dre, Ricky, me, and another Cedric (not the one from the projects) all went to the local store named Hudlin's. I remember the Hudlin's exterior was made of large natural stones. I had never seen a structure built like this before. It looked very secure like it was made to be bombproof.

The owner of the store was Mr. Hudlin, who would always stare us down whenever we entered his shop. It felt like we had stolen something from his store, so of course, walking inside felt like a dare. This behavior provoked us, and one day, we all dared each other to take something without paying for it. But the dare didn't end there. The catch was that you couldn't get caught. And guess what? The old guy lost!

After completing the dare, we all walked back to the block and started pulling out what each of us had taken from the store. I was the only one who got a honey bun. This made me win because I had the best thing that everyone wanted. I took a bite out of the bun and put the rest back into my jacket for later.

Once everyone returned home, I felt guilty for taking the honey bun from the store. Later that day, I went back to Hudlin's and returned the honey bun. The only thing is that it had a bite taken out of it. I felt better after returning it, though, and never stole anything from Mr. Hudlin again.

During this time, my biological father's girlfriend had bought me a brand new ten-speed bicycle for Christmas, and it was still in the box at my grandparents' house in St. Louis. After knowing he had bought me a present, I called him every week asking when I would get my new bicycle. Maybe he got irritated, so he stopped answering my calls.

Then I remembered my Uncle Bud and called him instead. Uncle Bud was basically my father figure growing up because he was the uncle who took me out and spent some real quality time with me. He and I would spend weekends together with his family, including his wife, Aunt Francis, and his children, cousin Miriam and cousin Kim.

I used to do house chores at Uncle Bud's house. I remember cutting the grass in his backyard, for which he paid me. I even took my first shower at his house because he was the only one I knew who had an actual shower in their home.

Aunt Francis was a good cook and made the best eggs ever. I loved it when she added cheese to the omelets. By this time, Uncle Bud's home was off State St. on Post Avenue. I loved spending time with Miriam and Kim. I made some beautiful memories with them.

When I contacted Uncle Bud and told him about the present my dad had bought, he decided he would pick me up on a Saturday and take me to St. Louis to get my bike. I knew I could depend on Uncle Bud. But fate was not on our side.

It was Friday evening when a big snowstorm hit the city. By Saturday morning, everything was covered in snow. After seeing the weather conditions, Uncle Bud said that it was not a good idea to go over to St. Louis. But I was quite stubborn. I didn't care about anything and furiously said to Uncle Bud, "You promised me. Now, you have to keep your promise."

At last, Uncle Bud gave in, and we were off to St. Louis to pick up my brand-new ten-speed bicycle. It was an awful ride but we had finally made it to my grandparent's house, who lived off West Florissant Ave on Clearance Ave.

We did not waste any time, as it had started snowing heavily again. We picked up the bike, still in the box, and put it in the trunk of my uncle's Chevrolet Impala. Bidding our goodbyes to my grandparents, we left the house.

As we were heading back over to the Poplar Street Bridge, it was difficult to drive. Uncle Bud had to slam on his brakes and make a sharp left turn to avoid hitting the car in front of us. We got slammed from behind and hit the guardrail that stopped us from falling into the Mississippi River. It was traumatizing.

Uncle Bud's car was crushed from behind, but thankfully, none of us were injured. Uncle Bud drove me home, and I looked at the trunk. It was damaged really bad; I did not even think about asking Uncle Bud for my bike. I felt bad the entire week, thinking it was all my fault. I should've agreed with Uncle Bud. Because of this I did not see my new bike for over a month.

Besides Uncle Bud and his family, Aunt Hattie was also an important person in my life. She was my grandfather's sister, who worked in downtown St. Louis. Aunt Hattie's real name was Harriet, but she changed it to Hattie, because she did not want to keep her slave name.

She had been arrested multiple times because she was African-American. Sometimes, Aunt Hattie would pass for being white because of her very light skin and her long, silvery, silky hair. She would get a pass from her white boss to work, but the cops would wait for her shift to end and arrest her in the back alley.

Aunt Hattie was the most God-fearing woman I have ever known. She was married to the Rev. Waters and they both were devoted Christians. Aunt Hattie used to get on her knees and pray for hours while me and my siblings sat in the other room listening to her pray. In my opinion, she was a religious woman and a disciplinarian. She was strict, too, and she did not like us chucking rocks into her front yard. If she caught us, she would not hesitate to grab a switch off the tree.

I remember one day, Rev. Waters took us to the shoe store to buy me, my sister, and my brother shoes. We were very poor, and they probably could not stand by and do nothing after seeing the shoes we were wearing. Later, I realized how kind and caring both of them were. They were the first religious people who ingrained the Word of God in us.

Chapter 5: A Father Figure
(I Finally Have a Dad)

I did not know what it was like to have a father, as I never had one and was brought up by my mother only. My mother, Gloria, has been the most hardworking woman I have ever seen in my life; she was born on October 21, 1938, in Proctor, Arkansas. She was the youngest among her ten siblings. My mother was only 20 years old when she got pregnant with my older brother, George Cason, and that same year, she married the man who was the father of her first child, also with the same name, George Cason. Her marriage lasted for hardly a few months; it did not even last a whole year when her husband deserted her, never to come back.

On April 2, 1960, my mother gave birth to her second child, my older sister Anita Hobson (Franklin). My sister Anita's father was murdered, and we never knew him. His murder was the only thing that we know of him. Then, finally, on November 5th, 1962, my mother had her third child kicking in this world, which was me. My biological father was Leodis Wofford, who never married my mother. My father had three children also, my older sisters, Sheri Exum and Pamala Grant, and my younger brother, Michael Wofford. In April 1974, my mother became a registered nurse and devoted several years of her life to serving the Veteran Administration Hospital and The Federal Records

Center Occupational Health Clinic in St. Louis, MO, until she retired in 1998.

My mother had accepted Christ at an early age and had been a member of Parks Chapel AME Church, Centreville, IL. My mother's best friend Gladys Porter, who attended nursing school with her, introduced her to a gentleman named Eddie Anderson Jr. My mother and Eddie dated for a couple of months, and then, on July 24th,1976, they got married.

Eddie Anderson, my stepfather, was born on March 13th, 1937, in East St. Louis, Illinois. Just like my mother, he was also the youngest one among his five siblings. He accepted Christ at Mt. Zion MB Church, was baptized at Friendship Baptist Church, and faithfully served as a deacon and member of the Busy Bee Auxiliary. He had been a scoutmaster for several years for the MT. Zion's Boy Scout of American Troop. Eddie, my stepfather, also had three children of his own who lived in Alton, Illinois with their mother.

My stepfather was a pillar for the community and by being a scoutmaster, he was always an advocate of trying to keep young boys on the right path during their teenage years and adulthood. My stepfather graduated from East St. Louis Lincoln High School Class of 1955. He further attended the University of Illinois and later worked and retired as a machine operator for Spectrulite Consortium, Inc. After retiring, he went back to work for Schnucks

Corporation. He loved traveling, fishing, hunting, and gardening. He often planted enough vegetables to share with his community, family, and friends. He was also known to be a faithful and dedicated member of the New Horizon Community Church, Deacon Emeritus, and had a deep love for music of all kinds. He was the kind of person who would deeply and dedicatedly invest himself in his family and the people he loved, hence living up to his devoted and faithful family man image.

My stepfather was a pious, God-fearing person and was also a disciplinarian who had a great sense of humor. He was the father that I never had but always wanted. He actually taught me what a father, husband, and Christian man is truly like. He taught me everything that he himself knew: fishing, hunting, driving, working on cars, and repairing things around the house so that the women of my house could rely on me for absolutely anything that they needed help with, and also, so that I was capable of handling things on my own no matter the time or situation. He was the man who came into my life like a ray of hope and pulled me out of the pit of darkness, eventually leading me to a path as bright as the sun, where everything made sense and made my life beautiful, saving me in the process. He came into my life when I was only 14, the time when the one thing I needed the most was a father figure, and he became that. God's timing couldn't have been more perfect.

I had spent my entire life without a father, and had seen my mother do everything on her own, so it was a bit unusual to see someone caring for my mother. Before my stepfather had come into our lives, I had never seen anyone care for my mom. When I saw someone doing it to her for the first time and how much ease and comfort she got from that love, support, and care, I could not help but fall in love with that man. The level of respect I had for Eddie kept on increasing as days passed, and I could not help but get inspired by him with every moment that went by. I wanted to become a man like him, as devoted and as loving as he was, someone who was always there for his family and super calm in handling everything and anything that was thrown his way. As a kid, sometimes I used to think that he was Superman, as there was absolutely nothing that he could not do, and he always had the solution to everything, no matter how difficult it may seem to others.

As happy and contented with my mother's marriage with Eddie, as I was, it was the opposite for my brother. To this day, I am unable to understand why he was against the idea of such an amazing and loving stepfather. I believe George was not happy with the presence of a new father figure in the household. He decided to quit school out of the blue, although he was a straight-A student. It was just one fine day when he decided to drop out of school and did not have any particular reason, nor did he give us any. My stepfather told him that he must go to school, get a job or he must leave the house, and to my surprise, he ended up leaving.

After dropping out of school and leaving home, my brother George joined the army and got injured in the boot camp, after which he had to come back home. Yet, nothing changed. So, my stepfather gave him the same option again; either he join a school and get a job or leave. Once again, he chose the latter and ended up moving out again. Our Uncle Bud took him in for a while after he got tired of him as well just living there; hence, Uncle Bud had to ask him to leave. So, George ended up joining the Job Core and never came back home after that. He has since been living in Seattle, WA. My brother, who I love dearly, has a beautiful family who all reside in the Seattle area now with their grandchildren.

Just like my brother George, Anita was also a straight-A student who graduated a year early from high school. She went straight into the workforce, moved out, and got her own place right after. Anita loved our stepfather and accepted him also. Anita actually became even closer with our stepdad after I left home. She always respected him and listened to him. Despite the difference of opinion that I and George had with respect to our stepfather, both of us were happy for our mother, and so was Anita. She and I were brought up in the shadows of our stepfather, who made sure that we grew up to be amazing human beings, and hence, it can be seen from the kind of person that Anita has become and the lifestyle that she carries. When Anita moved out and started working, she eventually went back to school to get her degree of BA. Later, she met her husband and has now been married for over 35 years, with one exceptionally smart son who is currently working on his PhD.

Eddie Anderson Jr. is the man that I would be indebted to till the day I take my last breaths because he was the person who made me into the man that I am today and provided me with everything that I needed and lacked in my life up until his arrival. Not only that but the way he took care of my sister and helped my mother in bringing us up and made Anita into the fine and responsible woman that she is today, I cannot be any less proud. Out of all that he has done, the thing I am most indebted to him for is the way he loved and cared for my mother. My mother was the kind of person who had an abundance of patience and possessed a kindness that others admired and loved. She found good in everything and everyone. She had an avid love for her family, friends, and the church. She was a sensitive yet strong person who always wanted to do the best for her family and was always on her toes for them. She would look at all the minor details in her relationships and would work on even the slightest of the issues, she was a perfectionist, specifically for her family. All of these traits that she had were reflected by her hobby; she was a miniaturist as well and had a passion for creating dollhouses and small discrete works.

She needed someone exactly like Eddie in her life, who would understand her the way she is and would look after her the way she tends to look after her loved ones. And it was exactly what my stepfather did; he looked after her like she was a little kid who needed attention, love, and care. My stepfather had become that one person for my mother to whom she used to go after spending the whole day tirelessly posing to be strong; he was someone she could and would get vulnerable with without the fear of abandonment or judgment. In early 2013, my mom was diagnosed with pancreatic cancer, and later, she transitioned early on a Sunday morning, on October 13th, 2013.

Things were tough for all of us after my mother passed away. However, it seemed to be the toughest for my stepfather, and that was when I actually got to see and realize how deeply he loved my mother. There was not a single day after my mom's death that my stepfather did not talk about her. For over seven years, there was not a single day that went by without my stepfather mentioning my mother in one way or another. Finally, on March 31st, 2020, on a Tuesday, my stepfather also passed away, and I strongly believe that he died of a broken heart, as he could not bear living without her any further.

Eddie came into my mother's life like a knight in shining armor. He helped her raise two teenagers into strong, independent, and fine individuals who are now settled in their own lives in the best ways possible. He took care of my mother the way she needed all those years of her life. It was like he had come to carry her in his arms to provide her with all the comfort that one could ask for, especially after the lifetime struggle that she went through. And most importantly, the way he stuck by her in her last days is something that I can never forget. He cared for her like a baby and would always be around her in case she needed something. My stepfather did not hire any caretaker for my mother; he looked after her all on his own. I am sure my mother must have passed away in a peaceful and comfortable state, for which I will forever be indebted to him. He was someone that I have always been inspired by, and if it was not for him, I do not think I could have turned into the man that I am now. He is someone who has.a major role in shaping my personality and making me into the man that I am now. has.a major role in shaping my personality and making me into the man that I am now.

My stepfather, Eddie Anderson, and my mother Gloria

Chapter 6: High School
(E. St. Louis Sr. High School - Home of the Flyers Class of 80)

It is a well-known fact that high school is a new world with different social norms, values, and rules, and when a student enters high school, they are stepping into a whole new world. This unique experience can either be an exciting or horrifying event for them. Some have to face bullies, cliques, and teachers who may not care about them. However, it is not the same for everyone; some even make memories in high school that last a lifetime.

When I look back on my school memories, it was definitely an exciting experience. It was a time for new friendships and getting used to a new environment. After grade school, I attended Wirth Junior High School in Cahokia, Illinois, where I spent my 7th and 8th grades. I remember being the skinniest kid there, the same as in my primary school. However, being skinny and short did not stop me from going out and trying for sports teams. I even managed to make the basketball and baseball teams.

Although I wasn't a starter, I loved being on the team roster for basketball. I remember that whenever we made the roster to play that week, we got to pick out our shoes. Back then, the school used to provide us with game shoes, which were Chuck Tailors All-Star. One day at basketball practice, another teammate and I had a collision that knocked my four front upper teeth back into my mouth. They were at the back of my mouth, and blood was spraying everywhere. The school contacted my mother, and that evening, I experienced the worst pain I had ever experienced in the dentist's chair.

At the time, I didn't know I was getting these really big metal braces implanted in my mouth. I still clearly remember the day they were implanted and the day they were removed because both times happened to be one of the worst experiences in my life. I had to wear the metal braces for almost a year.

Another memory I have from middle school is attending an interracial school for the first time. At junior high, my school consisted of 50% black and 50% white students. So, safe to say, it was quite the culture shock. The integrated environment brought with it some racially-charged fights, but since I played sports and was friends with guys from all backgrounds and ethnicities, I didn't engage in the fights that took place in the hallways.

After junior high, I attended Cahokia High School in Cahokia, Illinois, for one year, where I spent the ninth grade. Once again, I was the skinniest of the bunch.

It goes without saying that being in top physical form is imperative if you're going to be an athlete. After all, you're going up against the best of the best, and your team expects you to win. Unfortunately, I didn't quite fit the mold. However, despite being thinner than all the rest, it was a wonder how I could hold my own against the bigger boys.

Eventually, I also got into the football and track team and played tennis as well. While tennis and track went off without a hitch, football was a challenge, mainly because it was hard to get a uniform and equipment that would fit me. Everything was big on me, so I had to make modifications so that my uniform would not fall off me.

On the track team, I ran the 440, 440 relays, long jump, and pole vaulted. As an admirer of sports, I also wanted to bring back the school mascot (Comanches), but the Indian Comanche suit was too large for me.

From that time, I vividly remember being on a football practice drill and competing with the others while being the smallest on the team. One time during practice, I was so exhausted that I threw up in front of the head coach. Everybody started laughing and making fun of me, but the head coach stopped them and said, "If half of you had the heart that he has, we would be a much better team." That was the day I truly felt like I was part of the team.

It was between the 8th and 9th grades that my mother married my stepfather, and we moved from Elmijah Homes, 702 West Avenue, Centreville, IL, to 3528 Bond Avenue, East Saint Louis, IL. So, our parents had to drop my sister and me off at the bus stop in the old neighborhood and then pick us up from the same bus stop after school. However, the arrangement wasn't working for us, so after the 9th grade, my parents gave me the option to either go to Lincoln High School down the street on Bond Ave or E. St. Louis Sr High (East Side) across town. I went with East Side.

My choice concerned my parents because of the history of violence on the East Side, but it did not matter to me because everyone knew the girls at East Side were prettier than those at Lincoln High School. Therefore, East Side it was.

Switching schools from Cahokia was a confusing time as East Side began in the 10th grade. Therefore, my classes as a sophomore were all mixed up with senior courses. Since I was one of the shortest and skinniest people in the school, people often approached me in the hallway, asking if I was in the right school because they thought I belonged in middle school.

There were obvious differences between Cahokia and East Side. First of all, and to my shock, about 99% of the students in Eastside were black, with only about two white students in the entire school. Apart from that, East Side had a strict dress code, while Cahokia did not have a dress code at all, and if they did, they did not care about it. At East Side, you could not have your hair braided; it had to be combed. Also, your shirt had to have a collar, and your clothes had to be ironed and neat. It was like night and day compared to the Cahokia. Undoubtedly, the administration at East

Side cared about how their students looked and carried themselves.

As I came from Cahokia High School, where I played multiple sports, I thought I would be playing sports at East Side too. With that thought in mind, I tried to get on the East Side's football team and got selected. However, once again, I could not find any uniform or equipment that would fit me. I remember looking at the other candidates, trying out for the team, and thinking, "These dudes do not look like students; they look like grown men." It was almost always lost on me that they were seniors while I was just a sophomore.

I was confident that I could do it, so at the first football practice, it was my turn to get in the center and have some physical contact with other players during the drill. Other than my size, I had all the necessary skills. However, size mattered equally, and all I can remember is getting knocked out when the ball came toward me.

When I came to, I saw Coach Shannon looking over me and asking, "You okay, son? You okay?" They stood me up, and Coach Shannon asked me to head back to the school, take my uniform off, and wait for him in his office.

As I waited for him in his office, I thought about how I could convince him I was good at the game. As I was thinking about what went wrong and where I made a mistake, Coach Shannon walked in.

The coach stated that it was not a good idea for me to go back out there, trying to make the team. However, he gave me an opportunity to still be a part of the team by offering me the chance to be a trainer. That's when I became a trainer in my sophomore year, assisting Coach Stallings. Unfortunately, that year, East Side played for the State Championship but lost. I never went back to the football team as a trainer after that.

The next sport I tried out for was the basketball team. Unfortunately, when the first roster came out with the names of the players who were cut from the team, mine was at the top. Basketball was the last sport I tried out for at East Side because they were on a different level than Cahokia. As I stated before, I was one of the skinniest and smallest students in the school during my sophomore year, so the stakes were never in my favor.

I loved attending East Side; what was so unique about it was that you could be you. Since Cahokia was half black and half white, you were always kind of pressured to stick to your side when it came to style, music, and who you hung out with. However, since we were all black at East Side, you could just be you. For instance, we had black cowboys, rockers, nerds, scholars, and gangsters; people were free to be whoever they wanted to be and hung out with whomever they wanted to hang out with. That's why I loved attending East Side.

Another significant event of my life that I remember was the day when I was shooting craps with Buddy and Reggie at the back of our high school. The police rolled up on us behind a Wonder Bread truck, so we all ran toward the cafeteria to blend in with the other students inside the lunchroom.

However, looking at us trying to get back into the school, no one got up to open the door. All our peers in the lunchroom simply sat there and watched as the police patted us down and threw us in the back of the police car.

When the police officer was driving us away, he asked me if I was Eddie Anderson's son, and I replied yes. To my surprise, he drove us to the front of the school and told us to get out of the car, warning us that if he ever caught us again, he would take us straight to jail. I believe he must have been one of my stepfather's Boy Scouts in the past for him to show such generosity. Safe to say, my friends and I no longer shot craps at the back of the school again.

After getting out of the police car, we walked back into the school, thinking we were going to get caught by one of the principals. But no one was in the hallway, so we went to the cafeteria, where Buddy started cussing at the other students for not letting us in when we were running from the police.

Moving to the new neighborhood, I got to know all the kids fairly quickly because my stepfather was the local

Scout Master, and I had joined the scouts too. That's when I met my new group of friends; Michael McCoy, John Robinson, Reggie Bell, Cortez Branch, Michael Parks, Vernon Warren, Travis "Buddy" Williams, Lacelle Porter, Patrick "Blue" Patterson, Gary Howell, Luther Parker, Michael Young, and Robert "Robbie" Porter. We were around 13 or 14 when we met each other. I was also friends with Edmund Jones and Tyrus Young from the neighborhood.

These people were a significant part of my life during my next three years of high school. Just about all of them lived two blocks away on Trendley Ave. We also hung around each other's houses and the local swimming pool at Lincoln Park next to the Mary Brown Center. We also used to hang out around the grounds of St. Regis Catholic Church. It had a basketball court in the back and a huge lot of fresh-cut grass to play baseball and football.

At that time, I was in the Boy Scouts Troop 478, and we were the only all-black troop enrolled at summer camp. Our summers were usually spent at Camp Joy or Camp Vanderbilt. Our campsite was always far from the main camp, where all the cabins and cafeteria were. I remember walking past other empty, very clean campsites that were not assigned to anyone. On the other hand, when we got to our camp, it looked like it hadn't been used in years. We had to cut down weeds just to set up our tents. However, my dad said nothing; he was just happy that we could attend summer camps.

Summer camp happened to be one of the most racist instances I have ever experienced because the other troops hated us and made sure we knew it. But it brought us all closer together because we had to watch each other's back. Even after being treated unfairly, one thing is for sure; every campsite we left was in excellent condition when we packed up.

I still remember and cherish the most memorable day of my Boy Scout years: trying to get a skill award for canoeing. Everyone had to pair up for this competition, and I was paired with Blue. Blue was the tallest and darkest in the group, and everyone called him Blue because his skin was so dark that it looked like dark blue sometimes.

Anyway, Blue and I got into the canoe and started paddling out to the middle of the lake. When we got to the middle of the lake, our next task was to flip the canoe over, fall in the water, turn the canoe back over, get back in the canoe, and paddle back to shore. When it came time to flip the canoe, Blue remembered that he couldn't swim that well and changed his mind about the skill award in canoeing.

However, I had my eyes set on that award and was not going to let him rain on my parade, so I started to flip the canoe over while Blue threatened me by letting me know what he would do to me if I flipped it over. He started cussing me out and told me not to flip it, trying to come at me whenever I tried. He was holding on for dear life and still threatening me about what he would do to me once we got back to shore; I had never laughed so hard before in my life.

Eventually, we were able to turn the canoe over; we got back into the canoe and paddled back to the shore. As soon as we got out of the canoe, Blue was so angry that I had to leave that place immediately. I ran as fast as my legs would carry me because he was chasing after me.

I kept running until Blue ran out of air. I then had to dodge him for the rest of the day until it was chowtime. And thankfully, by that time, Blue had cooled off. It has been 44 years since that incident, and he has never thanked me for helping him get the skill award in canoeing.

This is just one of the hundreds of stories I can share with the readers about the Boy Scout Troop. I had a great time in the Boy Scouts, and we loved cracking jokes and making fun of each other.

As I was growing up, my parents were frugal with their money, so in high school, I started my first job as a busboy with my friend, Buddy, in a notable steakhouse to earn some money and pay for my expenses. The steakhouse was called Miss Hulling's. At 16, I used to catch the bus after school to my job. But how much can one earn by clearing tables? My hourly busboy salary was $3.10.

Miss Hulling's was a famous steakhouse, and all the big shots used to come there. I still remember a night in 1979 when I saw one of St. Louis's first black female news anchors, Robin Smith, having dinner with the youngest mayor in the country, Carl Officer, the mayor of E. St. Louis.

I took hold of the golden opportunity and asked him for a job in E. St. Louis so I wouldn't have to catch the bus every day over to St. Louis. The mayor said, "Absolutely!" and asked for my number. Needless to say, I never got the call.

The tips customers used to leave on the table had to be divided between busboys and waiters; all the waitpersons were older white ladies who were supposed to give us ten percent of their tips. However, I used to see the number of tips left on the tables, and I was sure they were ripping us off. So, Buddy and I started taking some tips off the table to make up for the difference. When those waitresses confronted us about shrinking tips, I confronted them about getting ten percent of the tips. That was our last day working at Miss Hulling's.

Being jobless was not an option, so Buddy and I applied at Stouffer Hotel after leaving Miss Hulling's. We were hired as the housekeeper's personnel five days a week from 5:00 pm to 10:00 pm at an hourly rate of $3.10. We were mostly in charge of removing trash from the hallways, cleaning the trash chute on the ground floor, and being available when guests requested a refrigerator or ironing board.

Since I was getting paid the minimum wage, I started selling the items I found in the "Lost and Found" at high school. I soon became popular in high school as the person who could get anyone anything they needed. You could say I became a mobile convenience store for my fellow students in high school.

I remember carrying a backgammon case all the time while a senior in high school, as all the items people asked me for were in the backgammon case. Watches, rings, earrings, fancy ink pins, and anything else that I found – everything would be in there. I also used my backgammon case to shoot craps under the bleachers between classes, lunchtime, and high school football games.

During my high school years, back in the 70s, it seemed like everyone was smoking Marijuana - at least in my world. It was so common back then that it was considered normal to experiment, and most of my friends were doing it.

There is no excuse for smoking Marijuana, and I would not make any. However, I will simply say that it helped with my ADHD. Smoking a small amount of pot actually made me feel calm and relaxed in the classroom. Moreover, my grades started to level up. Before that, it was very difficult for me to remain attentive throughout the class; hence, my grades also suffered.

However, when I started experimenting with Marijuana, my behavior got better, and I even made the honor roll for the first time.

I have to mention here that I was never a pothead like some of my peers, who stayed high all the time. I only used to take a small hit before school and another at lunchtime. Other than that, I rarely smoked pot, except maybe at some "basement" parties my friends used to throw. Even then, I would only take one hit when it was being passed around the group.

I always chose to buy my Marijuana in bulk instead of the nickel bag my friends were buying. Since I was business-minded, and I always had more than I needed, I started selling single joints, and boy, was it supply in demand. I had jocks, band members, scholars, gangsters, cheerleaders, and even a teacher as customers, but I will not mention any names. As I mentioned before, people approached me for all kinds of things. Therefore, I became a mobile convenience store for my fellow students in high school for their drug needs.

Marijuana was very high in demand, so I started keeping singles in my trusty backgammon case. My parents, of course, did not know about this. I even had to hide my senior autograph book from my family, as a lot of fellow students mentioned, and showed gratitude for my services in it.

I was good at hiding the Marijuana business from my parents. All they knew was that, along with my grades, my behavior was also getting better. Therefore, they never could have thought that I was involved in such a venture. Nevertheless, certain bad habits have to be left behind, so I did the same once I graduated high school.

When it came to my love life, I had a crush on Bridgette Williams. She was my best friend, Travis "Buddy" Williams' sister. She was my closest friend in high school, as we were in the same grade. She knew I had a crush on her, but I'm sure a lot of guys did. She was the most beautiful and intelligent girl in the school. However, she only dated guys older than her who had already graduated from school.

However, her dating older guys didn't matter to me as long as I got to hang out with my friend, and boy, we did. Since we only lived a couple of blocks away, we always hung out or spent hours talking the night away on the phone. I could tell Bridgette anything, and she could tell me anything without worrying about it getting out.

By the time senior year rolled around, I had fallen completely in love with Bridgette, and she knew it, but I was not up to the standards when it came to men she dated. However, that didn't stop us from hanging out. We used to skip school together, hang out at my house, and sometimes hang out downtown in St. Louis. I would try and give Bridgette jewelry, but she never would take it. I think the reason she never accepted any such presents from me was that she didn't want to create problems between her and her long-time boyfriend.

Some of my favorite memories revolve around the time I spent with Bridgette. I remember going to a dance with her at the Mary Brown Center. It was a slow jam, and we danced to our hearts' content. After getting off the dance floor, I heard my friend Blue teasing me, saying, "Ooo Wee, y'all look like y'all was making love on the dance floor." I told Blue to mind his own business.

I imagined what it would be like if Bridgette were my girlfriend. But even though I was in love with her, she always tried setting me up with other girls. And yes, I did date different girls in high school. So much so that when it came time to ask a girl to go to the prom, they all stated the same thing, "No! You are not going to stand me up on prom night." But one girl did say yes - it was Emma Thomas, and we spent a beautiful evening together.

A picture of me from prom with Emma Thomas

During this time, there was always something going on in my new neighborhood. I remember two brothers, Nukie and Pig, who moved to our neighborhood and became known as the neighborhood bullies. If someone said something they did not like, they wouldn't hesitate to knock that person out. They wouldn't stop beating them even after they fell unconscious!

Criminal activities in my neighborhood were an almost daily occurrence; bullying, stealing, and killing were the norm there. I remember a robbery in which my friend Blue's sister's husband, Charlie, who was working the night shift, got shot while on the job at a gas station. He died on the spot.

Another incident involved me; I was with Buddy in our local Chinese food joint, which we used to call Rice House. It was located on 29th and Bond Ave behind Blackmon's Liquor Store. We were picking up shrimp and fried rice when two men came into the rice house with their masks and guns. They started shooting at the roof and told us to get out of there.

Buddy and I started running out of the store with our heads down so they would think we did not want to see who they were. As we got out of there and started running down the alley, we heard shots and turned around, and it looked like they were beginning to shoot at us. So, we ran into a random backyard and crossed the street until we were back in our neighborhood.

These instances were not uncommon in my neighborhood. Each year at East Side, there was always an empty desk, and other students used to say that someone got killed last summer. During the school year, we always heard of one of our fellow students getting shot coming out of their home.

Right before I left for the Marine Corps, our neighborhood's local postwoman was raped and murdered just a couple of blocks from my house on Piggott Ave. We all knew her, and every person in the neighborhood said they knew who did it, but no one came forward to reveal the name. Eventually, however, the person behind the rape and murder was caught.

Whenever we went to a club like the Regal Room or skating at King skating rink, someone would get into an argument and start shooting up the place. It was not unusual to hear about people getting killed in E. St. Louis. Fortunately, I left E. St. Louis in June 1980 before crack cocaine hit the streets. I heard it got even worse after that.

As it was common in my neighborhood to get robbed and get death threats, I was about to get one too. During that time, I also picked up playing dice, and as it became my hobby, I found myself playing with one of the Original Gangsters (OG) in the neighborhood.

I took him for $70.00, and people started to talk about how a young punk had taken his money. After this, Buddy warned me and asked me to watch out for him because he started telling people he would take me out and get his money back. So that made me look over my shoulders every day until I left for Marine Corps Boot Camp.After graduating high school on May 29, 1980, it was now time to look forward to the future, possibly away from the crime and violence in E. St. Louis.

Bridgette Williams with Blue and his dog Beauty running in the background

Bridgette Williams

Cedric Cason

Chapter 7: United States Marine Corps

(No Turning Back)

While I was still attending high school, I signed the paper and gave my oath to enlist in the United States Marine Corps on February 11, 1980. The funny thing is, I actually intended on joining the Air Force. When I reached the recruiting station, I met all the recruiters, who happened to be good friends. I got to know that when one was short of meeting their monthly quota, another recruiter would send them one or more of their inductees. That was what happened to me.

While at the station, I saw the Air Force recruiter talking to the Marine Corps recruiter, and the next thing I knew, the Air Force recruiter was telling me that my test score fell just below the Air Force standard. However, I qualified for the Marine Corps. He then suggested that I go and talk to the Marine Corps recruiters. I did just that and that is how I ended up joining the Marine Corps, and honestly, I have no regrets. I guess it's true what they say; whatever happens, happens for the best.

***

It wasn't easy getting my family on board with my plans of enlisting in the Marine Corps. I was only 17 when I enlisted, and while my stepfather had no real problem with it, my mother was a whole different story. It took a lot of convincing, but she eventually gave in. However, it was my stepfather who signed the contract, officially allowing me to join the Marine Corps.

I distinctly remember the oath being administered, almost as if it was yesterday. Oath forms the bedrock of what the military is willing to fight for. It was a joyous occasion, and although it is part of the ceremony, it is far more than a simple gesture or a formality.

Embracing the oath, I stood straight with other recruits, all standing facing the front of the room. A marine officer entered the room and said that he was going to recite the oath to all of us and that we had to repeat it after him. We raised our right hands and began to repeat after him.

It seemed as if time stood still. I paused and reflected on the words I was saying, feeling a strong sense of patriotism and a sense of belonging to something bigger than myself, and at that moment, I felt invincible.

I thought I would be defending the framework of the nation; I might have to go far from safety but I would play my contribution in saving my country. I chose to join the Marine Corps, and the oath I embraced, the promise to be a part of an elite group that defends their country, made it official.

Finally, on May 29, 1980, I graduated high school. It was exciting for me, a chapter of my life closed, and I was ready to move toward a new beginning. On June 3, 1980, the day before we went off to boot camp, a marine recruiter picked up, and my old friend from junior high, Brian Frierson, and drove us to a hotel in downtown St. Louis.

I wondered why they picked us up and made us stay at the hotel the day before shipping us off to boot camp, but I figured it was because people changed their minds about joining the Corps at the last minute, perhaps due to a sense of nervousness or fear of what was to come.

When we entered the hotel, it was mostly filled with high school kids who were also awaiting to be shipped off to different branches of service, such as the Army, Air Force, Navy, and the Marines the next morning.

This was an important event in my life. I was about to go far from my home, family, and friends. I hadn't had a chance to meet my friends before leaving, so I saw an opportunity and called them that evening. To my surprise, they all showed up at the hotel within an hour to see me off and say goodbye, as I was not going to meet them for a long time. Lacelle, Robin, Buddy, Reggie, and Blue, the whole gang was there.

I don't remember much from that evening, but I vividly remember that everyone was having a party on the floor where my room was. The whole floor was occupied by the boot camp recruits; all doors were open, with everyone was enjoying themselves. There were bathtubs full of ice, fruit punch, and Everclear. With 95% alcohol by volume, the Everclear was shockingly strong. It is not meant to be consumed straight, as just one shot can make a person sick. It is intended to be diluted with other drinks, so we had to mix it with the fruit punch. Everyone filled their cups from the tubs and drank the fruit punch mixed with Everclear.

The next thing I remember is waking up the following day with the worst headache I have ever experienced in my life. All my friends were gone, and most of the other recruits were still passed out in their rooms or out on the hallway floor. Hangovers are rough; the more you drink the night before, the more severe the headache the morning after. It took three days for me to get over the hangover.

With a raging headache, I got on a Boeing 747 with Brian, that was headed to San Diego, California, to attend the United States Marine Corps (USMC) boot camp. It was my first time on an airplane and I felt a little fuzzy sensation in my head, yet it felt incredible taking off in a plane for the first time.

On day one of boot camp, a bus led us to the Marine Corps Recruit Depot in San Diego. As soon as the air brakes hissed, our hearts beat faster, our breaths became shorter, our palms started to sweat, and the bus that was filled with hopeful recruits was unified by the fear of the unknown.

As soon as we got off the bus, the yelling began, with the drill instructor ordering us to get off the bus and stand on the yellow footprints. The yellow footprints are where the marine journey begins; it is more than just paint on the ground. This is where we are transformed from civilians to recruits. That is also where we had our first taste of what was to be expected by the Marine Corps training.

We got a briefing on how to stand in a position of attention with our heels together and arms fixed by our sides. Stepping on those yellow footprints, I thought about how countless marines had stood on those very same yellow footprints.

At the yellow footprints, we had to repeat another oath after the drill instructor. After that, we got our heads completely shaved while the buzz of hair clippers drowned out the yelling of drill instructors.

We were then ordered to climb into bunks in the barracks, and I remember rubbing my shaved head, thinking what the hell did I get myself into? However, at the same time, I was comfortable and relieved that I no longer had to keep looking over my shoulder for the OG who was out to get me.

At this point, my eyes were heavy with sleep and the lingering headache from the hangover. At one point, finally, I fell asleep.

The next morning, every recruit received their uniforms and boots, along with other essentials, in the receiving barracks. When I got my boots, they were size 11, although I had asked for size 7. When I went over to ask for the correct size, the old white man in charge told me, "Keep going, boy, you got what you got," and that was that.

All enlisted service members were required to live in the barracks during basic training. A few days were spent preparing the recruits for "pick up," which is when we were sent to our platoons. This was the highly anticipated moment for recruits when we finally got to meet the drill instructors with whom we were going to spend the next several months training, molding, and eventually becoming Marines.

After spending a couple of days in the barracks, they asked us to march to our squad bay to be handed off to our Drill Instructors. Our Platoon #2048 was in the Second Battalion, Echo Company, and our Senior Drill Instructor was SSgt. Berridge and the Junior DI was Sgt. Derosier.

Marine Corps Boot Camp was life-changing for me. Being 5'8" and weighing 113 lbs., I was yet again the skinniest recruit in the platoon. However, the training there taught me that I could do anything I wanted despite my size.

The first thing that I received from my Drill Instructors was a "Double Ration Tag," which I had to put on my uniform. The tag meant that I would receive a double ration of food on my tray when I went through the chow line so that I could gain weight. However, it was the other way around for the overweight recruits. They received the "Diet Pvt" tag, which meant to reduce their food intake. Therefore, they would only be served salad and cottage cheese.

Marine Boot Camp is extremely challenging, both physically and mentally. We had to undergo strenuous physical training, and the difficulties of this process were presented to every recruit. It was not enough to simply endure everything; I had to persevere and push through to make even the slightest difference.

While training, I got challenged to a fight by another recruit, who I knocked out in front of the whole platoon. After that, no other recruit tried to challenge me. That's what I call street knowledge, "show people who you are straight out of the box."

Back then, the Marine Corps Boot Camp had three phases, the first phase was at Marine Corps Recruit Depot (MCRD), San Diego, the second phase was at Camp Pendleton, and the third phase was back at MCRD, San Diego. The first phase mostly consisted of yelling and screaming and breaking recruits down. We were pushed to our physical and mental limits so that our resilience could be tested. We lost most of our platoon during the first phase as the recruits surrendered to the tough training. I, on the other hand, thought that the first phase was fun, mainly because no one was looking to try and kill me.

***

While I was safe from the clutches of the OG, the same could not be said about the residents back home. After I left for boot camp, Blue would keep me up to date with the happenings back home, more specifically, who died or was murdered.

One call I can never forget is the one where he informed me one of my old girlfriends had been stabbed to death by her own cousin in the kitchen of their home. That really hurt because even though things didn't work out between us, we were still on good terms and would see each other whenever I came home on leave.

That news was the final nail in the coffin; I knew I was never ever going to return to E. St. Louis.

***

Coming back to training, the second phase started when they moved us to Camp Pendleton. At Camp Pendleton, we learned how to fire weapons, throw grenades, land navigation, and other things that were related to being an infantry rifleman. I breezed past this phase as well, as I did very well with the MI6, all thanks to my stepfather, who taught me to fire weapons.

On the last day of the second phase, we had to march ten miles with a 70-pound pack on our backs. We were being led by our Senior DI, and while marching, the recruits started to fall back, which caused a gap in our ranks. I knew it would be hard for me to catch up with the other recruits if I fell behind. Therefore, I went around the other recruiters and kept up with the Senior DI. When we were halfway up what is still, to this day, called "Mount Motherfucker," the Senior DI stopped and turned around; the rest of the platoon had fallen back about 50 yards. He looked at me and said, "What the hell are you doing here?" And I replied, "Following you, sir."

We waited for the rest of the platoon to catch up, and when they did, we began to march to the top. However, this was only the first three miles, and we had to complete another seven miles to go after climbing "Mount Motherfucker."

When the ten-mile march was over, all the recruits, including me, sat on the ground with our packs on our backs. I remember we had to remove our boots so the medical staff could inspect our feet. The medical staff was already there, waiting on us to finish the 10-mile march. Like everyone else, I got my turn to get my feet inspected. I remember that when I took my right boot off, the skin at the bottom of my foot came right off.

My feet hurt for the whole week, but I was not giving up that easily; I wasn't going to let that stop me from completing the second phase. However, fate was not in my favor that day. When the medical staff inspected my feet, they noticed that my foot was in a bad condition; not only was it infected, but I was diagnosed with cellulitis. It is a bacterial infection that causes swelling, redness, and pain in the infected area.

They immediately put me in an ambulance and took me to the Reginal Naval Hospital in San Diego. For a week, I was in the hospital with an IV in my arm and hooked on antibiotics. However, the day I got discharged, I got back to MCRD as I was determined to complete my training.

Upon my arrival at MCRD, they asked me to report to the Second Battalion Headquarters. I got to the Headquarters and went looking for Platoon 2048. After locating the barracks where the platoon was assigned, I went to the DI Sgt. Derosier. He was sitting in the DI's duty hut at his desk.

"What the f**k are you doing here?" Seeing me there, he stood up and yelled at me.

"To complete recruit training, sir!"

"Cason, you failed the second phase. You got to go back to Camp Pendleton and redo the second phase," DI Sgt. Derosier insisted.

"No, sir, I completed the second phase, and I am here to complete basic training with platoon 2048," I stood my ground.

He thought I was being stubborn, so he stated again that I failed the second phase and dialed the phone at the company office. Standing outside the Duty Hut, I heard DI Sgt. Derosier talking to someone in the Echo Company Office. Then he asked to put Sr. DI SSgt. Berridge on the phone. He informed the Senior DI that I was standing in front of him in the barracks, trying to get back in the platoon.

"Are you sure, Senior?" I heard him ask before he hung up. He then told me to go unpack my stuff and said that I was lucky to have a Senior DI who fought for me to stay with the platoon. At that time, all I knew was that there was nowhere in hell that I was going back to Camp Pendleton to do the second phase of training over again.

When my platoon came back from chow, they were all shocked seeing me there and excited as well that I was back in the platoon. The week I was recovering happened to be swim tank week. It was something I had been looking forward to since I was a great swimmer; it was a real shame that I had missed it.

Upon his return, the Senior Drill Instructor called me to the Duty Hut. When I went there, his first words to me were, "What the hell happened to your foot?" I informed him about the wrong-sized shoes that they were four sizes bigger than my actual size. I further informed him that I had asked for a size 7, but the uniform distributor made me take a size 11.

He was infuriated and ordered me to grab my boots and follow him. I followed him to the clothing warehouse, and we had a stern conversation with the workers there. After that, the warehouse worker handed me a brand-new pair of size seven boots, and then we left.

Coming back to the barracks, the Senior asked me if I could swim, to which I said, "Yes, sir." He inquired how I knew how to swim; I informed him that I had earned a skill award in swimming in the Boy Scouts. The next thing I knew, I was a first-class swimmer in boot camp.

I also became the head "House Mouse" in the platoon. There were four of them responsible for the logistics of the platoon. My duty as a House Mouse was to make sure that we had all of our gear and knew where to retrieve the gear when we needed it. Luckily, thanks to our Senior DI, we were never short of any equipment, while all the other platoons kept coming up short of their supplies.

I used to think that I brought some of my talents from E. St. Louis to the Marine Corps boot camp. In the third and final phase, I became a leader in our platoon; not the Guide or Squad Leader, but a leader within the platoon. Moreover, when it came to promoting some recruits within the platoon, I was selected by the Senior Drill Instructor to meritoriously go from Private to Private First Class and get my first stripe. It was my first promotion toward becoming an integral part of the Marine Corps.

I remember before completing boot camp when I was in the third phase of my training, I wrote a letter to Bridgette. I came clean and informed her that I was in love with her. I expressed my feelings and informed her that I wanted her to leave E. St. Louis and come with me to my next duty station. However, I never received a response from her.

Finally, one of the best days of my life arrived, and I graduated from Marine Corps Boot Camp; I was a marine. I remember telling Brian as soon as we graduated that I would run toward the seabag, grab it, and get the hell out of this Depot before someone changed their mind and held us back in the camp.

So, that is what we did; we grabbed our seabags and got directly on the next bus to the airport. We reached the San Diego Airport and while heading down the escalator, we saw that the Senior Drill Instructor was standing at the bottom of the escalator. Our hearts dropped to the floor after spotting him because we thought that he was there to take us back to the boot camp. However, when we came to know that he was there at the airport to take a flight, we felt relaxed and went to a bar to have a beer.

Me as a 17-year-old Marine

Chapter 8: My First Duty Stations
(29 Palms, Camp Pendleton)

After graduating from boot camp and before reporting to our first duty station, where we were to be trained, we were sent home for a week. I wasn't aware of what my duty would be until I completed the boot camp because when I signed up for the Marine Corps, I also enlisted myself on an "Open Contract." This meant I would not know what my Military Occupational Specialty (MOS) would be until I completed boot camp.

Most of the people who went in on an open contract normally got assigned as a (0311) infantry rifleman, which we called the "grunt." So, imagine my surprise when I was given the MOS as a Communication Electronic Center Marine (2542), which is now known as a Defense Message System (DMS) Specialist. The duties of MOS 2542 included operating teletypewriters, optical character readers, tape transport, and terminal consoles, as well as correcting, retrieving, and logging in messages. In simpler words, I was going to be a glorified typist clerk.

The school for communications was at Marine Corps Communication-Electronic School, Marine Corps Air Ground Combat Center in Twentynine Palms, aka 29 Stumps, the largest Marine Corps base in the United States, located in San Bernardino County, CA. I was glad that before I reported to 29 Palms, I got a whole week to spend with my family and friends back home.

Coming home after boot camp felt weird. Everything I remembered seemed smaller; my bedroom, my home, and even the town of E. St. Louis. Once we landed, our recruiter picked and Brian Frierson from the airport and dropped us home. He dropped Brian, and I remember telling him I would catch up with him later. Unbeknownst to me, this was the last time I saw him. Brian got assigned the MOS as Motor T, meaning he drove trucks in the Marine Corps, and we never crossed paths again.

As soon as I got home, I was excited to meet my friends and family, especially Bridgette. I knew my friends' group would be hanging out in our old spot, the St. Regis Catholic Church Field. I went there to surprise them. Everyone was happy to see me, but it did not feel the same as it used to be, and I think the reason was that I started looking at things differently after boot camp. I didn't care about getting high anymore or worrying about where my next hustle was going to come from. I was a changed man after boot camp. And so, the small talk got pretty old pretty quickly.

I excused myself and told the crew I would catch up with them later as my whole attention was on Bridgette – I intended to meet her as quickly as possible. After leaving my friends, I headed to Bridgette's house and knocked on the door, and there she was, pretty as always. She opened the door and gave me a beautiful smile and a hug to greet me.

Bridgette welcomed me back home and asked me to come inside. As I entered the house, it seemed like we were the only ones in the house, and I was excited to spend some alone time with her after so long. Unfortunately, that plan went down the drain when her sisters came out from their bedrooms, and all of them welcomed me. After some time, however, they returned to their bedrooms.

Finally, we were alone, so I took the opportunity and ask Bridgette whether she had received my letter, to which she replied, "Yes, I did." I was happy to hear that but worried when her demeanor changed as soon as I asked what she thought about the letter. She stared directly into my eyes and said that she thought the letter was cute, but she was never leaving E. St. Louis, ever. She further said it was her home. Why would she ever want to leave her home?

"This is it for you, E. St. Louis?" I asked as I was stunned by her response. Bridgette confirmed that she did not intend on ever leaving E. St. Louis. Something did not seem right; I could tell that something was wrong with my friend, but I decided to drop the topic.

I spent the rest of the afternoon telling her about my boot camp experiences and what I was going to do next. Bridgette, on the other hand, had no vision for her future, and accepting this was very difficult for me.

After that day, I did not hang out much with my neighborhood friends. Instead, I went to visit my family, including my uncles, aunts, and cousins.

Before leaving for Twentynine Palms, I met Bridgette again. We had a long conversation, but she did not feel like the same Bridgette I knew from high school. We used to be so close, and now the feeling was lost somewhere. However, I told Bridgette that my offer was still on the table and that if she ever changed her mind, she could always join me no matter where I was. With that, it was time for me to go and embark on a new journey in the Marine Corps, so I took my leave and boarded the plane that would take me to Twentynine Palms.

I arrived at Twentynine Palms on September 1st, 1980. The weather was scorching hot and extremely dry as it is located in the middle of a desert, and it was 110 degrees that day. When I reached my camp, all the students were assigned to open barracks, just like back at the boot camp.

The department where I was assigned, Communication Electronics, felt very boring. The requirement was to type 30 words per minute, and I could easily do that because I had experience typing in high school. So, although I excelled at it, it still did not interest me. It became a routine for me to be in a hurry for class to end so I could get out of my uniform and hang out either at the YMCA or the enlisted club.

One day at Twentynine Palms, I went to the enlisted club and met Anthony Johnson, aka AJ, from Detroit, Michigan. We instantly clicked and became good friends. Unlike me, AJ was not a student; he was permanent personnel who was stationed in the Supply Battalion at the base.

AJ and I started to hang out in the permanent personnel barracks. They had their own rooms, and AJ asked me if I wanted to use the extra bunk he had in his room. I immediately jumped on the offer so I could get out of the open barracks. I started staying in AJ's room at night and would come back to the student barracks in the morning for formation. It was obvious that other students were jealous of me staying in the permanent personnel barracks.

It wasn't easy being me at Twentynine Palms. Within the first six months of my being in the Marine Corps, I received three Non-Judicial Punishments (NJPs), aka office hours. It was a punishment for marines where they had to stand in front of the Company Commander as a punishment and give a statement about why they did what they did.

I remember my first NJP was for fighting with the "Fire Watch." The fire watch was a person assigned to guard the barracks at night while the recruiters were asleep. When I came back from AJ's place one night, the Fire Watch started asking me where I was, and I told him to mind his own business. The next thing I knew, we were pouncing on each other. Everyone in the barracks awoke because of the commotion and jumped in to stop the fight. The next morning, I received NJP for harassing the fire watch.

The second time I received an NJP was when I was walking with a female marine to the permanent personnel barracks. She was carrying a boombox, and the music was playing out loud. Someone on duty told her to turn down the music, but she did not follow the order, and I asked the guard to mind his own business. A lieutenant who was observing us approached me and asked for my name and rank.

I was on the report again for disobeying a direct order, and there I was, standing in front of the Company Commander yet again, within a week of my previous incident.

The third NJP I received was for fraternizing with a non-commissioned officer (NCO). I was hanging out in the permanent personnel barracks with a female Marine Corporal (CPL) in her room. Another CPL was there on duty and saw me entering the room. He came and knocked on the door. When she opened the door, he saw me sitting in her room. He asked me what I was doing there.

"Minding my own business," I shrugged.

He ordered me to leave the room, threatening to call the Military Police otherwise. As I had a habit of getting in trouble, I said, "Really? You don't have anything better to do except harass other people?" Safe to say, I received another NJP for that.

I found out after that incident I was not supposed to hang out with NCOs as a private first class. This was the third time I was in trouble, so my Company Commander asked me why I kept showing up in front of his desk. I stated that I was simply living with my half-brother AJ in his room instead of being in the open barracks with the other students.

The Commander eyed me from top to toe and then informed me that he knew AJ and that we looked like we were twins. However, he did not punish me this time, as I was just hanging out with my brother, and ordered me to move back into the student barracks.

Before he dismissed me, he asked whether we had the same mother, and I said yes, we did.

"I knew it," he said.

All three NJPs I received were due to altercations with well-known redneck marines who had a reputation for targeting black marines. For the rest of the time on the base, AJ and I fooled everyone into believing that we really were half-brothers.

While stationed at Twentynine Palms, AJ and I made friends with a couple of grunts who were also stationed there. Our group grew bigger and better, and the members were Brown, Shorty, AJ, and me. Everyone in the group was from Detroit except me. Every other night, we used to go to the enlisted club, and I remember people getting jealous of us. They would often challenge us to fights as well, which we always welcomed.

Therefore, I was involved in many fights at the club. The fights were increasing day by day so the club manager and owner got frustrated and kicked us out of the club despite the fact that we were not the ones who started these fights.

Being from E St. Louis, I used to bad mouth a lot, and denigrating the opponent became my habit, which resulted in fights. However, with Brown by my side, I felt invincible. I always stood next to Brown whenever we got into fights, as he was the strongest and biggest among us all. I knew my other friends also had my back as I was the skinniest in the group, still weighing only about 120 lbs.

Even though Brown was the biggest, I remember him as a gentle giant who would get completely drunk with just one bottle of beer. He was by far the most gentle and kind person I met during my time in the Marine Corps.

A month before we graduated, I wanted to escape from the MOS of 2542 Communication Electronic Center Marine and asked AJ how I could do that. He told me that the only way I could change my MOS was to flunk the class, and then they would have to give me other options for MOS. So, that was what the 18-year-old Cedric did. I intentionally flunked the course as I did not type 30 words per minute, which was the requirement of that course, and failed other finals as well.

Failing the class continuously made my instructor disappointed in me. He told me to get out of the class and that he knew what I was doing. So there I was again, in front of the Commander, reporting why I was failing the class. I did not lie and told him the truth that I did not want the MOS of 2542.

Although the Commander was upset with what I was doing, he could not do anything about it. So, he offered me two options, either Bulk Fuel Operator or Warehouse Clerk. Since AJ was in supply, I chose the Warehouse clerk.

Within the blink of an eye, I was ordered to leave Twentynine Palms and report to Camp Pendleton, Base Material Battalion, to start the warehouse school. Yes, there is such a thing as a warehouse school in the Marine Corps where marines get the forklift license and other logistical training.

In March 1991, AJ borrowed a car and dropped me off at Camp Pendleton, CA. There, I played baseball on the Battalion Baseball Team while attending warehousing school. Apart from that, my time at Camp Pendleton was mostly uneventful.

After graduating from warehouse school, I was told to report to the 3rd Marine Division, Okinawa, Japan, on September 5, 1981.

Before reporting to Okinawa, I went to visit my friends AJ, Brown, and Shorty in 29 Palms. I rented an old sky blue 1970 Nova Chevrolet from a rent-a-car company called "Rent-a-car-Cheap" on Oceanside Blvd. I had already informed AJ that I would be coming to meet them on the weekend so when I reached 29 Palms, they had prepared a going away party for me. My old crew was back together again, a reunion for the last time.

AJ had four tickets to a Lakeside and The Gap Band concert in Riverside, so we went to Riverside on Saturday and had a blast that evening. We enjoyed ourselves a lot and stayed the night in a hotel.

On Sunday morning, we were on our way back to 29 Palms. When we got to Yucca Valley, CA, I noticed some police cars were chasing us with their sirens and lights on. They surrounded our car and ordered us to pull over, which I did immediately. The deputies jumped out of the vehicle and pointed their guns at our heads, ordering us to lift our hands so they could see them. I was about to reach for the glove department to show them the rental papers when AJ stopped me and asked me to put my hands on the dashboard.

I got annoyed when they asked us to step outside the car, still pointing their guns at our heads. I yelled at them, informing them that this was a rental car that I got for the weekend. However, they did not care about what I had to say and ordered us once again to get out of the car. As soon as we stepped outside the car, they tackled us to the ground and handcuffed us.

Still yelling, I was trying to tell them that we did not do anything wrong and the car was rented and told them to check the paperwork in the glove department, but they were in no mental state to hear us out and just wanted to lock us up.

They threw us in the back of the police car, took us to the police station, and locked us in a room. One hour passed by, and we sat there helpless. A deputy then came toward the lock-up and unlocked the door. He walked us to the lobby and told us we were free to go.

When I demanded my rental car back, all the police officers started laughing. I remember one saying, "That's not going to happen, boy," before stating that the car I rented was reported as a stolen car. I got infuriated and asked him what that had to do with me and how I was supposed to go back to Camp Pendleton. That fell on deaf ears.

Huge laughter emerged in the police station once again and the deputy said that it was not their problem and asked us to get going. We left the station and tried to find a ride back to 29 Palms, as there was no chance the deputies were going to give us a lift anywhere, let alone all the way to 29 Palms.

As we walked down the street, I was boiling up with anger and was feeling burned up with what had happened to us. AJ tried to calm me down. He said something that I would remember for the rest of my life, "Cason, you don't know why God had them stop us. As far as we know, God could have saved our lives by avoiding a fatal accident up ahead. Remember, Cason, everything happens for a reason, so let's count this as a blessing and thank God that we are still alive."

This incident and AJ's words changed me into who I am now. I started thinking differently about each and every aspect and situation of my life after hearing those profound words.

However, I was still angry at the redneck deputies for making us walk miles to find a ride. I thought about how they could have at least given us a ride back to the base as they knew we were marines, but they were so egoistic that they laughed at us instead of helping us.

The next day, AJ managed to borrow a car from someone and drove me back to Camp Pendleton. I left Camp Pendleton and got on a plane to E. St. Louis where I spent a few weeks catching up with my family and friends before leaving for Okinawa, Japan.

At the Marine Corps Birthday Ball in 29 Palms, CA, 1980. AJ and I shaking hands

Chapter 9: My Duty Stations
(Okinawa, Japan)

During my leave, which I was spending in E. St. Louis, the only person I could think about was Bridgette. I was so eager to meet her that as soon as I was done unpacking, I went to Bridgette's house. However, when I reached her house, I was disappointed as no one was home.

Since my friend Blue lived just three houses down from her house, I went to meet him instead. Blue and I kept talking for a while, but whenever I asked him about Bridgette, he ignored my question. I kept asking him and he kept changing the topic and dodged my questions that were about Bridgette. I was desperate to know about her and annoyed by Blue's deflection, I stopped him in the middle of the conversation and asked him why he was avoiding talking about Bridgette.

"Ced, I don't want to be the one who tells you," Blue hesitated.

I was getting annoyed and asked Blue to tell me what was going on. Finally, Blue told me that Bridgette was gone.

"Gone? What do you mean gone? Is she dead?" I asked him cluelessly because he was not giving me a clear answer.

"No, she ain't dead, but her mind is gone," Blue tried to remain calm.

I asked him what the hell he was talking about. The words coming out of his mouth were not making any sense. Multiple emotions were coursing through me, scaring me to death; I was scared for Bridgette and what could happen to her. How bad was it? What did she get herself into?

As wave after wave of horrible thoughts went through my brain all at once, Blue finally broke his silence and told me something that gives me shivers to this day. He informed me that Bridgette was kidnapped and drugged. He said, "They put a needle in her arm and kept her for over two weeks." Blue then stated, "Ced, you don't want to know what they did to Bridgette during those two weeks."

I could not believe what I had just heard; I wanted this to be a nightmare, a short nightmare that would be over soon. But it was not, and I had to face the reality no matter how much I wanted it to be a terrible lie.

"What the hell are you talking about, Blue?" I screamed with tears running down my cheeks. "This is bullshit, I don't believe you. Where is Bridgette now?"

Blue's deafening silence was killing me. After what felt like ages, he finally said, "Ced, I'm sorry to tell you this, but Bridgette isn't the same anymore; she just walks the streets most of the time now."

"What the hell are you talking about?" I must have repeated this sentence several times, but I really did not know what the hell he was talking about and how something like that could have happened to Bridgette. Or maybe my mind just wasn't letting me accept reality.

I asked Blue where I might find Bridgette, and he told me the corner of 29th St. in front of Blackman's Liquor Store. After hearing that, I hastily jumped in my mother's car, which I usually used when I came back home and hit the peddle in hopes of reaching 29th St as soon as I could. I was driving fast, and as I was about to cross the turn to reach 29th St., I saw Bridgette walking down the street heading in my direction. I hit the brakes and immediately pulled over.

I screamed Bridgette's name, but she kept walking. I pulled up next to her and called her again. She then finally recognized me and uttered, "Ced, Ced, you made it back home!"

I got out of the car and looked into Bridgette's eyes, but her eyes felt empty, hollow, almost - like there was no one there. I held her shoulders and assured her that it was me, her friend Cedric. She looked at me again and repeated, "Ced, you made it back home."

Looking at her condition, I was worried and asked her to get in the car and let me take her back to her home. Without any argument or uttering any word, she immediately got in. As we were en route back to her place, she asked me if she could borrow $5. I couldn't say no to her and immediately pulled a $5 bill out of my wallet and handed it to her.

As I pulled over in front of her house, she immediately got out of the car without saying anything.

After dropping her off, I went back to Blue's house and told him everything; I told him he was right, that she was not the Bridgette I used to know.

After gathering myself after what I had just seen and Bridgette's condition, I asked Blue who were the guys that had done this to her, but he didn't know. He only knew that the kidnappers were from St. Louis.

All I remember after talking to Blue was getting back into my mom's car and crying and screaming. I remember yelling, "Why? Why Bridgette?"

My hatred for E. St. Louis increased tenfold after that, and I realized that I no longer wanted to come back to this place. All I wanted to do now was to leave as soon as possible.

The time I spent in E. St. Louis after that was miserable. I barely left my parents' house, and leaving that place was the only thing on my mind. I counted the days till I would be shipped off to Okinawa.

The day before my flight to Okinawa, I went to meet Blue. Driving by, I saw Bridgette walking down the street, so I pulled up next to her to say hi. But when Bridgette saw me, she said, "Ced, you made it back home."

'Maybe she has forgotten about our last meeting,' I thought.

Bridgette then asked me if she could borrow $5. I got out of the car and tried to talk to her, but she was not in her right mind. The Bridgette I knew no longer existed. So, I told Bridgette that I would lend her $5 one more time, but this would be the last time. She took the $5 and looked directly into my eyes, and I looked back into hers. Looking into her eyes, for a moment, I thought Bridgette was back, but she was not. She walked off, heading to 29th St.

I stood there watching her go to the path of hell. I cried because there was no hope left for her. I turned the car around and made my way back home.

The next day, I was on board the plane to Okinawa, Japan. However, all types of emotions were rushing over me — excitement for a new start, leaving behind my past life, but most of all, my heart was heavy bearing the sadness that Bridgette's misery gave me. I could not put an end to her thoughts no matter what I did.

***

I landed in Okinawa, Japan, with my eyes wide open in amazement and wonder. Everything was different here from back home. I had never been to another country before, and the changes were quite drastic. All the cars were smaller; they drove on the opposite side of the street, and it was very crowded.

After we landed, we saw buses waiting for us outside the airport. We got on the buses, which took us to a receiving barracks at Camp Butler. At the camp, everyone called us "newbies" because we were new to the island. My fellow marines were feeling homesick already, but I was not; I was just glad that I was far, far away from E. St. Louis.

Once we got settled in the barracks, the authorities there held a formation in the evening right before chow time. While we were in formation, they instructed us that since we were newbies, we were not allowed to leave the base. Therefore, we were restricted there until further notice.

After chow time, the first thing we did was leave the base. We jumped into a honcho (cab) and went to the exact place where they told us to stay away from, "BC Street." There were about eight of us, so we had to take multiple honchos and make a pact to stay together to ensure we all returned to the camp together.

When we got to BC Street, we were blown away by the women of the night houses and clubs who were trying to drag us into the club so we could buy them a drink.

Almost everyone wanted to go into a club to see a show, so we went to one to see a banana show. All I can say is that we not only saw the show but more than that. Walking out of there, we all had our minds blown. We had seen enough, so it was time to return to our base camp.

***

The next morning, I reported to Camp Kinser, where I was assigned to a Supply Battalion. However, when I went there, they assigned me to Consolidated Issue Point (CIP), Camp Foster.

So, I was back on the bus to report at Camp Foster. On the way to Camp Foster, a bunch of Okinawans was protesting at the main gate of the camp. They were holding placards that said "GI's GO Home" and chanting as loud as they could, "GI's GO Home."

Helpless to my nature, I could not resist and rolled down the bus window, sticking my head out of the bus, and yelled, "Send me home, send me home." Everybody on the bus started laughing. They said I was crazy, but I said, "I'm on their side; if they don't want us here, then send us home."

Unaware that the Japanese newspapers and news stations were also at the gate covering the protest, I landed in hot water. Apparently, I ended up on the front page of a newspaper. Within 72 hours in Okinawa, I was standing in front of the Commanding Officer, getting yelled at and receiving "Office Hours." The Commanding Officer restricted me to base for a week and warned me that I must not be seen in his office again.

***

My unit CIP was a local warehouse in the center of Okinawa that shipped supplies all over the Island to other Marine Corps Units. However, I was disappointed when I came to know that I had to live in an open squad bay again because I was an E-3 (LCpl). In Okinawa, if you were an E-3 or below, you lived in an open squad bay-like boot camp. Only E-4 (CPL) and E-5 (Sgt) were assigned individual rooms.

The people stationed there were mostly either gym fanatics, drank a lot and hung out in the clubs off base, or were devoted Christians who attended Church on a regular basis throughout the week. I might add that before I left Okinawa, I was in all three groups.

I was trying to be attentive now and tried to keep a low profile because I had gotten myself in trouble already. So, I stayed on the base most of the time and became friends with my bunkmate, who was a Christian, and all he did was work, eat, attend Church, and read the Bible. He used to attend church off-base, and I started attending church with him.

It still feels like yesterday when I gave my life to Christ and accepted Jesus Christ as my lord and savior at a Bible study. I had been attending church for a month, and on that pleasant Wednesday, Bible study was ending, and the pastor proceeded with an altar call. An altar call is when a pastor asks individuals attending the service or Bible study if they are willing to accept Jesus Christ as their lord and savior.

I remember my heart beating faster as I felt like someone was standing in front of me, and all I saw was a bright light. It was an out-of-body experience, a trance I fell into where I was floating outside of my body. I saw an altered perception of the world, and it felt like it lasted very long.

When I came back to my senses, I realized that I was still sitting at the Bible study, and people were staring at me. I did not know what happened or what I did, but I felt a love that I never had before, and I started crying and yelling, "Yes, Jesus! Yes, Jesus!"

It was at that moment I realized Jesus was knocking on the door of my heart, and I accepted Him as my lord and savior. So, I stood up and walked up to the altar to give my life to Christ.

The pastor asked if I accepted Jesus Christ as my lord and savior and if I believed that He was crucified and rose on the third day, and I said yes.

Two weeks later, on January 17, 1982, I was baptized at Maranatha Baptist Church, Okinawa, Japan, by Pastor Edward E. Gibson. Since then, I started feeling the Holy Spirit living inside me, and accepting Jesus Christ as my lord and savior in front of hundreds of people changed me as I dived into reading the Bible daily and attended Church and Bible study regularly.

Unfortunately, only two months had passed since my spiritual awakening, and I already started to skip reading the Bible and attending Church. I drifted from the right path and started hanging out with the other marines in my unit, who were mostly involved in drinking and visiting nightclubs off base.

Simply put, I did what Christians call "backsliding." I lost the path that was leading me to righteousness. Christ never turned His back on me; I turned my back on Christ. While I was backsliding, I knew what I was doing was wrong and the Holy Spirit was convicting me, and I still chose to sin. But God showed patience, and I am grateful for God's grace.

The two marines, aka brothers, I started hanging out with were Lee and Rivers; they used to work at a club called "Lido's Night Club." They both had been in Okinawa for a long time and had no plans of leaving any time soon. Both of them had Okinawan girlfriends and children with these girlfriends as well. They may have had a rack and a wall locker in the barracks, but they never lived there. Instead, they lived with their girlfriends in apartments in town.

Lee and Rivers were respected on the island, and I never saw anyone else getting the same respect as them. Lee used to race at night in town, and I remember him asking me one time to pick up one of the racing cars that he kept in his garage off base, and I happily obliged.

When we reached his garage, he threw me the keys to his car and asked me to follow him. When I got in the car, I discovered that it was a stick shift. I had never driven a stick shift before, but Lee gave me a two-minute crash course. I quickly grasped the instructions he gave me, fastened my seatbelt, and hit the peddle. Keep in mind that this was also the first time I had ever driven on Okinawan streets and the first time I drove on the left-hand side of the street.

It's been years since that day, but it still seems like yesterday. It was raining, and I had no idea what I was doing, but at least I figured out how to shift gears and kept my pace until we reached our destination.

Driving that car made me confident; I thought if I could drive a car I did not know how to drive and still reach our destination safely, I could do anything.

Some of my fellow marines were making a lot of money through the black market. They used to buy liquor at the exchange and sell it in town at ten times the cost they bought it. However, I had no intentions of indulging in the black market industry in Okinawa, so I kept my distance.

I started working at the nightclub where Lee and River were DJs and bouncers and worked at the door as well. Although I worked there as the door staff, I used to take over as the DJ when Lee needed a break.

Lee and Rivers liked me and looked out for me, so they helped in increasing my payroll. They even introduced me to other clubs that were exclusively for Okinawans and did not let other Americans in, not even military soldiers, but they let us in.

So, there I was with the OGs of the Island without a ride; the money I was making at the club had to be utilized now. I bought a brand-new moped for $2000 and signed up for the motorcycle school in Okinawa. Until I received my license, I did not inform anyone about the moped, and when I finally got my license, I picked up my brand-new Yamaha moped. I remember when I showed up at the barracks with my moped, everyone came running out to see it and couldn't believe that I had bought one. I believe I was the only marine on the base that had a moped.

**

Eventually, after some time, I got promoted to E-4 (CPL), which had many perks. Finally, life seemed to take a turn for me; I had enough money to buy the things I wanted, and I finally got my own room. I even bought a brand-new Kenwood stereo system with gigantic speakers and a top-of-the-line Cannon camera with expensive lenses. Watching me spend money so fast, Lee and Rivers warned me about overspending and that someone might get suspicious.

Soon after that, I was notified by the GySgt that I was selected to go on an exercise that would take me to the Island of Tinian for about six to eight weeks. The marines used to call this exercise a "float" because marines normally would have to sit at the bottom of a Navy ship to get to wherever they were going. However, as I was in supply, I got lucky and traveled in a C-130, an American four-engine turboprop military cargo transport aircraft.

The flight to Tinian became an unfortunate event for us as we had to make an emergency landing on Guam because we had lost half of our engines. As we landed, one of the crew officers informed us that we were flying on only one engine. Therefore, that is why we had to stop in Guam. Although I did not want to sit in that plane again, I had to, and eventually, we reached Tinian.

For the people who are not aware of the history of Tinian, it was the launching point for the atomic bomb attacks against Hiroshima and Nagasaki, Japan. Tinian is a beautiful island with smooth rock pools that the ocean waves splashed into and kept full of warm ocean water. We would catch crabs and boil them in hour helmets. I remember the crabs being very salty, but they were better than the sea rations.

We stayed on the island for eight weeks, and we had to drink the dirty water available there as long as we stayed there, which gave all of us diarrhea.

Before coming to Tinian, one of the old Vietnam brothers, who was now a civilian, told me that I would find Marijuana growing wild on the Island. He suggested I bring it from there and sell it in Okinawa as it was expensive there but high in demand. However, I had left that life in E. St. Louis and refused, telling him that I would not be selling any more drugs. Not for sure if Marijuana grew wild on Tinian, but everyone was selling it, but I did not partake.

Gladly, eight weeks passed by, and I returned to Okinawa. I continued what I was doing there before, hanging out with Lee and Rivers and other locals who worked at Lido's Nightclub. That was when I fell in love with Okinawa. I was learning all the traditions and visiting local restaurants that were unknown to other military personnel.

Being friends with Lee and Rivers had its perks; we were allowed on the beaches of the Island, where only Okinawans were allowed. As time passed by, they all became like a family to me which made working at the nightclub even more fun as we really enjoyed being around each other.

Often, after closing Lido's Night Club at 2:00 am, Lee, Rivers, and I used to go to Napoleon's Night Club on BC Street, which was behind Kadena Airbase and usually closed down around 4:00 am.

I remember closing the club with Rivers one rainy night while Lee had already left for Napoleons. As Lee had already left and there were no other means of transportation, Rivers asked me if he could jump on the back of my moped for a quick ride to Napoleons.

As my moped was made for one rider, Rivers had to sit on my compartment case on the back of my moped. That night, we had been drinking a lot, and I admit I was a little intoxicated, which we usually were. The reason behind our always being intoxicated was that we used to get free drinks when we were working.

We were headed to Napoleons when all of a sudden, a Japanese Police DUI Check Point appeared, and the police started waving at us to stop. They asked us to get off the moped and started yelling that this bike was only made for one person and that I was breaking the law by riding with a passenger.

The trouble did not end there; the police could smell alcohol in our breaths. It was at that moment that they figured we were drunk and started yelling at me about how I had been drinking and driving. They immediately took out the keys from the moped and ordered us to get in the police car.

As I got in the back of the police car, I watched a police officer drive my moped behind us to the local police station.

Once we got there, they asked us to get out of the car and took us into the station. They made us sit down on the long wooden stool in front of the front counter. I admit I was scared to death that I was going to get arrested and charged with a DUI. Even though Rivers told me to stay cool and relax, I could not.

The police officer who was driving my moped came into the station, placed the keys on the front counter, and went to the back with the rest of the officers. I looked at Rivers, stood up, and said, "I am outta here." I remember Rivers looked at me like I was crazy, but I went to the counter, grabbed my keys, and ran out of the station. I jumped on my moped and took off, leaving Rivers behind in the station.

The next thing I know is that I was scared to death that the police were after me. In an endeavor to avoid them catching me, I drove into the old neighborhoods that had the smallest streets, trying to make it back to Camp Foster.

I remember rolling my moped a couple of times because the streets were slick, and I was driving too fast. But eventually, I made it to Kitamae, which was a small town right outside the Camp Foster gate, at around 4:00 in the morning. I just waited and watched the gate to see if any police officers were waiting for me to approach the gate. However, I did not see any police cars or officers, so I drove to the gate. As I reached the gate, the Military Police came out of the Guard Shack and let me into the base.

Considering the current predicament I found myself in, I could not understand what to do. The first thing that came to my mind was to run, so I immediately drove my moped to our barracks, drove it into the laundry room, and pushed it into Mama-son's supply room.

Mama-sons were Okinawan elderly women who worked in each barracks, cleaning and ironing our uniforms and polishing our boots. They worked in our laundry rooms, and the marines paid them on a weekly basis. After parking my moped in Mama-son's supply room, I went to my room and went to sleep.

The next day, I stayed in the barracks waiting for Rivers to show up, but he never did. I remember it was Sunday, and I stayed in my room all day, avoiding stepping out.

On Monday, I had to report to work and step out of my room. I could not hide there anymore. When it was time to report to work and I was just about to go out scared to death, Rivers came yelling and laughing that he had never seen anything like that before in his entire life. I remember him telling everyone, "Cason is crazy."

He told everyone about what had happened Saturday night, and I explained to everyone who was thinking that I was crazy that the only thing I was trying to do was get my moped back.

Needless to say, I did not leave the base for over two weeks. After two weeks, I couldn't take it anymore and decided to go back to work at Lido's. I had no idea what was going to happen to me when the Japanese police saw me, but it was better than staying in the barracks for the rest of my time in Okinawa.

Eventually, I drove up to Lido's Night Club on a Friday night nervously. When I reached there, I saw police officers standing around, maybe because there were multiple clubs on the same corner. As I drove past the police officers, one of the officers saw me and pointed at me. Before I knew it, all the officers were pointing at me and started laughing.

Yes, all they did was point at me and laugh like I was the joke of the party. However, I still was not able to figure out why I was not arrested, but I remember that it was like the weight of the world was lifted off my shoulders.

I parked my moped and went into Lido's. Lee was standing right in front of me. He looked at me and shook his head. I was happy that I was back at work and everything was normal.

Months passed by, and I enjoyed myself in Okinawa, making friends like family. After that, for the last months that were left for me in Okinawa, all I did was stay at the base most of the time, go to the gym, and work out.

The thought that the Japanese police may have a warrant against me crossed my mind all the time. I was not sure if I would be able to leave the base. I thought maybe they were just waiting on me to try to leave the Island with my arrest warrant.

At last, I received orders to report to Camp Lejeune, NC. When it was time for me to check out, I checked out of all the required stations, including the Military Police, and all was cleared for me to leave the base.

On my last day in Okinawa, I gave my moped to Rivers because I knew he had a liking for it. He was pleased to get the moped, and I felt that I owed him and Lee a lot for taking me into their family and caring for me.

The thought of being arrested at the airport still haunted me, so I felt relief when I boarded the plane. I remember saying, "Thank you, LORD!" when the plane took off as I could finally breathe without any fear of being arrested.

Chapter 10: My Duty Stations
(Camp Lejeune)

Camp Lejeune is one of the largest Marine Corps training facilities in the United States, which consists of approximately 109,047 acres in central North Carolina. I had to report to Camp Lejeune on October 4, 1992. So, I left Okinawa and went back to E. St. Louis on leave before reporting to Camp Lejeune.

Coming back to my hometown, I could not stop thinking about my childhood best friend, Bridgette. I was worried about her; I still could not believe what she had been through, and there was nothing we could do to give her justice and punish her kidnappers.

The thoughts of Bridgette led me to her brother, Buddy. After meeting with him, I came to know that she had moved to Washington Park with her boyfriend. When I heard that she had moved on with her boyfriend and that she was safe, I was a bit relieved and moved on too.

***

While in E. St. Louis, I ended up buying my very first car from my mother, which was a 1975 Chrysler Cordoba two-door coupe. The first thing I did was detail the car from both exterior and interior.

I started with car vacuuming and washing. For deeper cleaning, I had to remove certain parts of the car to get into the cracks and crevices that had never seen the light of day. I had to apply specialized products as well to enhance the car's appearance. The final result came out as fruitful as expected and the car looked and smelled brand new, even though it was aged over a decade.

The truth is, the process of detailing the car was much more complicated and time-consuming than I had thought, but I was appreciated for my work. I remember my stepfather saying he had never seen that car that clean from the inside out when he first saw it.

Before I could be a proud owner of the car and leave for Camp Lejeune, the car started to run hot. I asked my stepfather to help me with the problem, but he humbly denied my request for help, saying, "It's your car now, and you must figure out what's going on with it and causing it to run hot. And you have to figure out how you are going to fix it."

So, I went to figure out the problem and opened the car's hood. After going through each detail, I figured out that the car needed a new thermostat, but I did not dare ask my father for help. So, without any help, I bought a new thermostat and installed it in the car myself. It felt as if I had conquered something big; it was a great feeling not just to own a car but also to be confident that I could repair it.

I pampered the car and cleaned it inside out again before leaving my hometown. The car was good to go and I was ready for a solo road trip in my Chrysler Cordoba. I was off to Camp Lejeune the next day; the gold applique surrounding the dash shone brightly when I drove on the roads of Illinois. This was the longest road trip I ever took. As a matter of fact, it was the first trip where I drove myself.

Finally, I made it to Camp Lejeune and boy, what an eye-opening sight that camp was. It felt like the entire base was on steroids; everyone had high and tight haircuts, boots spit-shined, and uniforms squared away.

Seeing the competition, I knew I had to game up if I wanted to fit in. So, when they came to the receiving barracks looking for volunteers for Jump School, Fort Bragg, NC, I immediately raised my hand. However, they only wanted twelve volunteers, and as they were counting from the opposite end from where I was standing, I was the thirteenth one with a raised hand. This left me disappointed because I was confident that I was going to be one of the only marines in Supply MOS with Jump Wings.

I was assigned to the 2nd Maintenance Battalion, the 2nd Force Service Support Group. I reported to Battalion Headquarters to check in, but I was told that I would have to check in the field. The entire battalion was on a training mission in the field, aka "the forest," where they would have to live and operate in tents.

When I reached the field, the operation was coming to an end, and the battalion was moving back to the main base. So, I returned to the main base with them within a week.

My living quarters were located in the base at a place called "French Creek." Since I was a Corporal, I thought I would get my own room, but I was wrong. I had to live with two roommates, Rucker and Richardson.

Fortunately, Rucker and I got along pretty well, but Richardson was pretty much a loner. Both Rucker and Richardson were black, but Richardson was a bit different. He was very conceited and carried himself like he was better than the rest of the black brothers in the unit. I must mention that by the way he spoke, one could not tell that he was a black person unless they saw him in person. Thus, we used to call him the Bryant Gumbel of the group because he spoke so properly.

I was glad that I was not assigned to the warehouse with the rest of the Supply Marines. Instead, I was assigned to the (S-1) Battalion Administration Personnel Office and worked as an 0111 MOS, the Admin Clerk. I had to perform personnel, clerical, and administrative duties, which were better than having to be in a hot and musty warehouse. Moreover, I was fortunate enough that mostly the beautiful female marines were Admin Clerks. I liked being an Admin Clerk and became fond of my work.

Camp Lejeune was the most racist base that I had ever been stationed at. There was a rule that if you were black, you could not go out in town and have fun, so there was nothing much to do at the camp.

The racist pamphlets of the Ku Klux Klan, aka KKK, were all over the place. The KKK had a long history of violence; it was the oldest and most infamous hate group in America, and Black Americans had been the Klan's primary target.

I remember my Battalion Sergeant Major instructing all black marines, forbidding us from utilizing the back gate at Camp Lejeune because of the KKK activity in the area. I was stunned to hear that; I thought we were free citizens of America and were free to go where we pleased, and that is how it should be. Anyhow, out of concern for our safety, all of us kept our distance from the back gate.

I remember another time when the Base Commanding Officer (CO) gave the order to all marines stations at Camp Lejeune and surrounding bases that there would be KKK rallies in town, so we must stay away from both the main and back gates. He further instructed us not to participate in the rallies. I remember thinking, "Wow! Really? Do you have to give orders for Marines not to participate in KKK rallies?"

However, I eventually figured out why he had to give that order when I was confined to the base with others watching the rallies on the TV. We saw a few white marines participating in the KKK rallies. "Damn! I cannot wait to leave Camp Lejeune," I whispered to myself.

When weekends came around, all the black marines tried to leave the base, especially when we had three or four days' leave on the weekends. So, people who owned cars went to "Swoop Circle," a place on our base where we could meet and go on rides to Washington, D.C., Richmond, VA, Baltimore, MA, and Philadelphia, PA.

Every Friday afternoon, the cars would gather at Swoop Circle, and the car owners would announce where they were headed and match the passenger marines who wished to go there as well. The car owners would drop the marine passengers at the local bus station in that city, and on the way back to the base, they picked up the same marine passengers at the same bus station. We swooped out of Camp Lejeune like birds, hence the nickname "Swoop Circle."

The whole arrangement worked perfectly well for everyone, especially the car owners, because you could get the passengers to cover the gas cost and other expenses as you received anywhere between $25 to $50 round trip per passenger.

As for me, I used to just flip a coin and decide where I would take a trip that weekend just to get the hell out of Camp Lejeune. I remember the adventurous trips I took to Howard University during the Greek Picnic Celebration and to Richmond, Virginia, where I attended a concert with Prince, Time, and Vanity Six.

Not a lot of crazy stuff happened at Camp Lejeune, but there is one incident I will never forget. I remember the day when I saw military cars headed toward French Creek from my quarters. No one knew what was going on until we got to work. We came to know that one of the Admin Clerks whom I worked with had raped and then attempted to murder one of the female admin clerks.

Needless to say, we were all in shock, stunned to our bones, as we knew both of them. The marine who raped her was a loner, a young white man who had acid rock tattoos like Ozzy Osborne on his body. He tried to escape, but he was caught trying to swim across the French Creek. He received a 20-year prison sentence. That seemed like a long time, but that may have meant he could have gotten out of prison in 2004.

All I can remember about the poor girl who got raped is that she was almost strangled to death, and we never saw her again after that.

***

As time went by, Rucker and I were starting to get tired of our roommate Richardson complaining all the time. He complained about everything, our every move or noise. He kept accusing us of touching his things, coming into the room late, and making too much noise.

We had had enough of his complaints, so we decided to prank him. We set Richardson's clock two hours early when he was asleep. We wanted to give him a head start since he always wanted to be the first in the chow line. He set his clock for 5:30 in the morning, but we changed it two hours early, so the alarm rang at 3:30 am.

At both of these times, it was dark, so Richardson could not see the difference. Until he got dressed and went to the chow hall, we acted like we were asleep.

As soon as he left, we got out of our bunks and burst out laughing as we watched him going toward the chow hall two hours early to have breakfast. We could see the chow hall from our room, and it did not take much time for him to come back from there. We quickly got back into our bunks and pretended to be asleep, but Rucker could not stop laughing.

We got caught, and Richardson was very upset about what we had done to him. But Rucker and I burst out laughing again until tears came out from our eyes, and our stomachs started hurting. As we were laughing, Richardson said to us, "That's okay, y'all got me this time, but the payback is going to be a bitch." Hearing this, we knew that Richardson was angry at us because we had never heard him swear before.

However, payback never came, and Richardson received an Honorable Discharge as he decided not to re-enlist and went back home to attend college.

Rucker and I remained at the base and became even better friends. David Rucker was an entrepreneur and always had different ideas to make a fortune. One weekend, he showed me a way to become filthy rich. He was passionate about this idea, and after listening to him, I decided to join him.

His idea was to invest in Amway. It was a multi-level marketing company that sold health and beauty products based in Ada, Michigan. Even though I had never heard of it before, I joined Rucker because it sounded like a great idea to me, and Rucker was not going to leave me behind if he was going to get rich.

We spent the next few weeks in Washington, D.C., and Richmond, DA, trying to grow our business. We attended seminars of Amway where all the big shots presented on topics of how to get rich, how much money they had, and where they spent their money so that we could learn and keep dreaming of being like them one day. They recommended two books, "Think and Grow Rich" by Napoleon Hill and "How to Win Friends and Influence

People" by Dale Carnegie. We were invested in the thought of being rich, so we bought those books and read them. We also bought tapes by Amway bigwigs where they recorded how they earned their money.

I was glad that I met Rucker because it was because of him I got to know what it was like to want more out of life, to dream big, and to have a vision for the future of being successful. All the material, including the tapes, notes, and presentation, was helpful. Neither of us got rich from selling Amway products, but we both gained experience and underwent a lot of positive changes in our personalities.

In the same way that AJ at 29 Palms changed my thought process about situations and how God is in control, Rucker changed the way I looked at my future and made the best of the possibilities while believing in myself.

One day, Rucker was driving to Washington, DC, to give an Amway presentation. He was almost killed in a horrifying crash. We were told by the doctors that he might not make it, but he survived. About a month after his accident, Rucker returned to work. I remember him picking out glass from his skin after the accident. However, we became used to him doing that and laughed about it.

I recall one day at work, my boss, the Administration First Lieutenant, went through my personnel file and noticed that I was a first-class swimmer. He was extremely impressed with that and told me that he was supposed to assign someone to go on Temporary Assignment Duty (TAD) to Onslow Beach for six months during the summer for Lifeguard Duty, and the person had to be rated a first-class swimmer. The Lieutenant then asked me if I was interested in the position, and I said yes. The next week, I had to report to Onslow Beach, 2nd Reconnaissance Battalion.

When I arrived at the beach, I discovered that there was only one black lifeguard, and the rest of them were white. The other black lifeguard was a returning lifeguard from the previous summer, so he knew everyone already. On the other hand, everyone looked at me like they were saying, "Who the hell is this skinny marine?"

Needless to say, I was put on reserve and never got an opportunity to be a full-fledged lifeguard. I was assigned to the maintenance crew for most of the summer. There were a few times I was called to lifeguard duty, and, to be honest, it was very boring and extremely hot sitting in that chair. So, I didn't mind being assigned to the Maintenance Crew because they had the freedom of strolling anywhere on both beaches.

Yes, even the beaches were segregated between Enlisted Beach and Officer's Beach. I was mostly assigned duty at the Officer's Beach as all the officers' wives came to the beach, and I found them attractive. The summer went well, and finally, the time came to report back to my permanent unit back at French Creek.

Once I reported back to my unit, I was assigned to a supply position in the warehouse to drive a forklift. I met a guy named George Washington there, and we got along well. He was in love with his high school sweetheart, and they got married. Over time, we had gotten so close that he made me his best man.

Walking at my base camp, I saw my old girlfriend I met at 29 Palms when I was in Communication Electronic School. Seeing her at the camp, I was both stunned and excited. We started hanging out together, and I stopped going to Swoop Circle on weekends. Instead, I spent my weekends traveling with my old girlfriend to different places, including Disney World and Atlanta, GA.

Time with her passed by quickly, and she was stationed in Okinawa. Hearing the news of her moving to Okinawa devastated me. I remember Rucker asking me what I was going to do, and he could not bear my answer. I said to him, "I will ask her to marry me." Rucker lost his mind listening to my reply and said, "You must be crazy. You two have been together for just a couple of months." But I did not care as I was in lust/love.

Rucker tried to talk me out of it, but I did not want to lose another woman in my life like I had lost Bridgette. So, I asked her to marry me. She did not take it well at first as she was shocked and hesitant, but eventually, I persuaded her, and in just a couple of days, we got married.

Only Rucker knew I was getting married, and he was my best man as well, standing right beside me when I said, "I do."

Her and I were married for only two days when she had to leave Camp Lejeune for Okinawa. When she took off on a plane, leaving me behind at Camp Lejeune, I wondered whether I had made a mistake. I knew this marriage would be hard to work on when both of us had to live separately. So, I requested Washington, DC, to waive my overseas control date.

It had taken a month for my request to be approved and another month for me to receive orders to move back to Okinawa.

Rucker and I moved into an apartment off-base during these two months because we had faced enough racism and harassment by the redneck SNCOs on base. It was so heinous of them to target all the black marines about the pettiest things.

Before coming here, I did not know that I'd have to face such blatant racism. Although cultural diversity is one of the greatest things as a nation, sadly, racism and hate still exist. It is an awful thing to be on the receiving end of racism. Often, it can be tempting to direct your feelings of hatred right back at the racist, but the most powerful thing you can do is to take the action that is comfortable to you. So, this is what I did; I took an action that was comfortable for me and moved away from the base.

Chapter 11: Returning to Okinawa
(Betrayed and Confused)

The idea of a married couple living apart from each other after being married for only two days is a highly uncommon notion. A marital relationship is bound by the concept of family and living together under one roof. Just like any type of marriage, it takes a steadfast commitment to make a long-distance marriage work.

The baseline is that I loved my wife and wanted to make the relationship work no matter the distance between us. So, it happened after my wife left for Okinawa. I immediately filed a request to move there, and a few months later, my request was approved, and I finally received orders to return to Okinawa.

I landed in Okinawa on November 30, 1993. The day marked five months since I had last seen my wife. When I landed in Okinawa, it seemed like I never left, and to be honest, I was happy to be back.

I was assigned to the 1st Marine Airforce Wing (1st MAW), Marine Wing Communications Squadron 18 (MWCS-18) on Camp Foster this time around. It was a good day.; I was in Okinawa, I was about to meet my wife after five long months, and most of all, she was stationed on the same base, Camp Foster.

After arriving at the base camp, the first thing I did was locate my wife. Seeing me there, my wife was glad that I had made it over to Okinawa and that we were finally going to be together. The first thing we did together was buy a car. After that, we went on the hunt for an apartment and took the first available one.

However, choosing the apartment in haste was a mistake because it did not have a Western toilet. We got to know the difference between an Eastern and Western toilet once we moved into that apartment. The toilet in the apartment was built into the floor, and a person had to squat over it to use it.

The toilet was unacceptable to both of us, so we started searching for another apartment immediately. After living a month in the apartment, we finally found one with a Western toilet and moved there as soon as we could.

When I checked in to my post at Marine Wing Communications Squadron 18 (MWCS-18), a Gunnery Sergeant (GySgt) went through my file and noticed that I had worked as an Administration Clerk. GySgt Hunt was the Administration Chief for the Squadron and asked me if I would like to go back to working in the office environment, and I said 'yes.'

I loved being an Admin Clerk, I was responsible for managing the Files and Directives Section. I had to maintain all the Standard Operational Procedures (SOPs),

Marine Corps Orders, as well as Publications from Washington, D.C., Navy Publications and Orders, and all the latest changes to the Publications and Orders to include all the latest bulletins from the Commandant of the Marine Corps.

After working for a few days as an Admin Clerk, a fellow marine informed me that in every inspection we received from the Commanding General Inspection Team, the Files and Directives section always received an unsatisfactory score and was the worst in the whole 1st Marine Aircraft Wing.

I became concerned and asked GySgt Hunt how to fix the problem. However, asking him did not prove to be of much help as he instructed me to throw everything out and start ordering new SOPs, Publications, Orders, and Bulletins. Moreover, he ordered that everything must come in a file with an order sheet to show the date and time it was ordered. So, I followed the commands and worked hard on them for three months straight to keep up with the updated files and directives. Eventually, my hard work paid off, and the Files and Directives department was updated and in much better condition.

While in Okinawa, I started missing my first moped, which I had bought there, so after moving to town, the first thing I did was buy a new moped. This moped was a Yamaha as well, like my first one, but it was bigger and more spacious and could carry another passenger.

In the first few months back in Okinawa, I met a lot of new people as well as old friends who still remembered me, some were from Camp Foster, while others were from my first visit to Okinawa.

I remember that after a month of moving back to Okinawa, I met Lee and Rivers. Just over a year, they had gotten married to their girlfriends and had a happy family. Lee had been discharged from the Marine Corps while Rivers was still enlisted, waiting for his contract to run out. Moreover, I was surprised to know that Lee had opened his own nightclub in Okinawa, which was listed in his wife's name. Lee let me DJ in his club from time to time while Rivers was still working at Lido's Night Club.

Meeting them after a year and seeing them settle with their happy families was an exhilarating experience that I will cherish forever. It was like a long-awaited wish fulfilled because we had the same long-lasting bond of friendship as we had a year ago.

I stayed in touch with Lee and Rivers over the years. While Lee's nightclub was a successful hit, Rivers got in trouble with the law and landed himself in Naha Jail, where I visited him to bring him cigarettes and gum. Eventually, Rivers was released from jail and immediately sent back to the United States.

***

Since I was married now, I was happily living off-base with my wife. Things were going great until one day, someone saw my wife's picture on my desk and asked, "Why do you have my friend's girlfriend's picture on your desk?"

I remember getting stunned and telling him that he must be mistaken because she was my wife.

"Then, why has she been hanging out with my friend on another base for the last three months?" he asked sarcastically.

Hearing someone say things like that about my wife boiled my blood, but I remained calm and said again that he must be mistaken.

After getting home, I informed my wife about the incident that happened at work. My wife went quiet; her silence made me suspicious, and I started to think about the stuff the man had said about her hanging out with another man for three months.

"What the hell was he talking about?" I furiously asked her, and that is when she admitted that she had been hanging out with someone but that she had ended it as soon as I arrived in Okinawa.

I got knocked out of the air for a moment as I could not believe that she had cheated on me. I started yelling at her, "How could you do this to me?! You are supposed to be my wife!" My heart was shattered. I was embarrassed and ashamed that my wife was known around the island as someone else's girlfriend. I didn't know what else I was supposed to do. I didn't know how to react to all this as this was a huge shock to me.

A week went by with me giving my wife the silent treatment. While she kept apologizing, I kept giving her the guilt trip, reminding her that she was my wife while she cheated on me.

However, after a week, I realized that the only thing that was hurting was my manhood, the idea that my wife was hanging out with someone else, and people knew about it. But, to be brutally honest, I also practiced infidelity once my wife left Camp Lejeune, so who was I to judge?

Both of us were young, only 21 when we got married. Moreover, we were separated for the first ten months of our marriage after being married for only two days, so I should have seen that coming.

I realized that she loved me and that I also had some skeletons in the closet, so I tried to make our marriage work. Without telling her anything about me cheating on her with someone else in Camp Lejeune, I forgave her, and we both moved on as we were willing to give our marriage a chance.

After a couple of months, my wife got pregnant. After hearing the news, we were overjoyed. One minute, we were happy, and the other, we were overwhelmed and tearful. We were truly over the moon and couldn't wait for our little bundle of joy to arrive.

The next day, I went to my office and started distributing cigars to announce the news to everyone. That day, I also vouched that I would quit smoking because I did not want to smoke in front of my child.

As the months went by, I was promoted to assisting admin chief, and it was my responsibility to check in all the new marines to the unit. One morning, I received a bus full of new marines and noticed a black marine, a Lance Corporal (LCpl), while he was getting off the bus. I asked him where he was from, and he said, "South Philly." I asked him his name, and he said, "Anthony Moore."

I looked for his name in the roster and checked him off while noticing that his MOS was a Field Wireman, aka a Marine Electrician, who "bugged" people. At least, that was what I thought anyway.

I could not resist and kept an eye on him for a while and noticed that he was a loner. One of the Master Sergeants in the Squadron approached me and told me that he was looking for a new driver for the 1st MAW Commanding General, who happened to be General Frank Peterson, the first African-American General in the Marine Corps.

Furthermore, the MSgt entrusted me with finding the right candidate for the position. He informed me that the candidate would be sent to the Headquarters to be interviewed by the General himself. It took me about two seconds to choose LCpl Anthony Moore as he was way more mature than the other marines in the Squadron. Moreover, he was alone most of the time and barely talked to anyone, so I did not take him for one to gossip.

I told the MSgt that I had the perfect candidate for him, and he said that he wanted to interview the candidate first before sending him to the Headquarters.

However, LCpl Moore's reaction was quite the opposite of what I expected. When I notified him that I recommended him to be interviewed for the Commanding General's driver position, he got angry at me and said he was not interested.

I told LCpl Moore that he had no choice in the matter; he was the only candidate from our Squadron and he would be interviewed with six other candidates from other Squadrons for the job. I also informed him that if he did not want the job, then he could blow the interview. Therefore, he agreed to go through the interview process, but unwillingly and with no intention of getting the job.

LCpl Moore did give the interview but did not seem hopeful about getting the job because when I asked him how the interview went, he told me that he didn't think he would get the job and they had not made a decision yet.

After interviewing LCpl Moore, the MSgt recommended that his interviewing process should be sent forward to be interviewed by the General. A week later, we got a request in our department to send LCpl Moore to the headquarters for another interview, and to my surprise and delight, he got the job as the Commanding General's driver.

I was proud of him and of myself as well to have selected LCpl Moore for the interview, so I made sure that I let everyone know that I had recommended him for it. The MSgt just gave me a nod and said, "Good choice."

When I saw LCpl Moore driving the car of Major General Peterson, the Commanding General of 1st MAW, I felt great and proud that I had something to do with him getting the job. I was even more proud seeing a black person driving a black General.

LCpl Moore was meritoriously promoted to Corporal as the Commanding General's driver. Realizing that he did not have too many friends, being the CG's Driver, I started inviting Anthony Moore over to my apartment for dinner and BBQs on weekends.

I believe the reason that my friendship with Tony was close was that no one in the marines could handle the liquor as we did. Whenever there were drinks at parties or gatherings, Tony and I drank loads of liquor. Even after everyone passed out or left the party, we used to open an old scotch, sit on my apartment's roof, and listen to Sade's Diamond Life Album, lots of Motown classics, and smooth Jazz.

***

One day, I was locking up the office when suddenly, a Major, who was the Executive Officer and the second in Command after the Commanding Officer, approached my desk and yelled, "Take down that got damn communist off of my bulkhead!"

I did not understand him and said, "Excuse me, Sir?"

"Take down that got damn communist off of my bulkhead!" He repeated while pointing to the picture of Dr. Martin Luther King Jr. I had put up.

Being a young Cpl, I was excited about the opportunity and the changes I could make with the position. I had taped the picture of Dr. Martin Luther King Jr. to the wall next to my desk. However, after getting scolded by him, I carefully took the picture off the wall and put it in my drawer.

To this day, I regret not standing my ground and disobeying another direct order as Martin Luther King Jr. was my role model, the person who stood for the equal rights of Black Americans when no one did.

Later that year, the Inspector General team conducted the semi-annual inspections of all the units within the 1st MAW. While my department, Files and Directives, was being inspected, the commanding officer and the GySgt were not expecting a positive grade due to the history of previous inspections.

However, when the results came, the Files and Directives section received an "Above Average Rating." Except for me, everyone was shocked and GySgt Hunt was amazed that I managed to bring the department a good score.

The Commanding Officer, LtCol. Williams, personally came to my desk to congratulate me and said that he was grateful and promised me that I would be receiving a Navy Commendation Medal for my effort.

I remember having a basketball tournament in Okinawa, which was held between other Squadrons within the 1st MAW. MWCS-18 was the underdog because we were at a disadvantage, being the smallest unit. Our team only consisted of eight players and SSgt Moore was our coach, a loud and intimidating coach who carried a hammer around.

We won the tournament with the help of SSgt. Moore, who threatened other players, upsetting many on the opposing teams. Also, as a result of my outstanding performance, I was voted the MVP as well as the high scorer of the tournament. I received my generic MVP trophy from LtCol Williams, who recognized me immediately and said, "You again! You really make our Squadron shine."

While receiving the trophy, a thought suddenly flashed in my mind, and I asked LtCol Williams about the Navy Commendation Medal that he promised me after the IG inspection. He assured me that I would be getting the medal. However, he never fulfilled his promise, and I never received the medal.

Just when I had lost all hope of getting promoted, I got promoted to Sergeant. I could not believe that I was promoted and went straight to GySgt Hunt and asked him how I got promoted, to which he replied, "You deserved it," and that was that.

I was grateful for the promotion, especially with me and my wife having a baby soon.

Time passed by quickly, and here she was, a pure little angel, our little girl, born in August 1984.

As we were overjoyed with the arrival of our little girl and the people around us were so supportive, we made our request for an extension in Okinawa for another year which easily got approved.

Both my wife and I were sergeants at the time and were a happily married couple with a child, living on Okinawa Island, and even took a vacation in Korea. We were known around the community and started getting to know the locals there. We were active in all the community activities, which also included picnics. I got my certificate in scuba diving as well.

I received orders to report to the 1st Marine Division, Camp Pendleton, CA. My wife, on the other hand, received orders to report at the Marine Corps Recruit Depot (MCRD) in San Diego, CA. Fortunately, both duty stations were within 60 miles of each other, and the Marine Corps considered us being on the same base. So, we were not apart at that time.

Our friends even gave us a farewell party the night before our flight to where we were stationed. Tony offered me a ride to the airport and even gave me a going away present, a fifth of Johny Walker Black. I opened the bottle immediately and drank with him on our way to the airport, and within a flash, the whole bottle was empty. As a result, I passed out on the plane and came back to my senses after landing in Tokyo, from where I had to catch a connecting flight to San Francisco.

I was back in the States a few days earlier than my wife as I had to pick up our brand-new car, a 1985 Toyota Celica Coupe Black worth $13,925, which we bought in Okinawa. It was shipped to San Francisco from Guam. So, I picked up the car from the dock and drove it to San Diego Airport, where I had to pick up my wife and daughter when they landed.

Chapter 12: Drill Instructor
(First Tour 1986 Through 1987)

In November 1985, we returned to the United States and settled in San Diego in a beautiful apartment we rented named Mira Woods Apartments, located in Mira Mesa, right off Interstate 15. My wife and I decided to settle there because it was between Camp Pendleton and the Marine Corps Recruit Depot (MCRD), San Diego.

A few days after moving there, we met a happy and beautiful couple, Lisa and Rodney, from San Francisco. Rodney was an aircraft mechanic in the Navy, stationed at Miramar Naval Air Station. We became close friends the day we met and still are.

My wife was assigned to the MCRD Communications Center, and our daughter attended daycare there as well. On the other hand, when I checked in at Camp Pendleton, I was assigned to the 1st Marine Division, 1st Tank Battalion, as the Warehouse NCO.

I was not fond of Tank Battalion; in fact, I didn't give it much attention as all I could smell there was diesel fuel overriding the fresh air. One of the many reasons I hated Tank Battalion was that they made us run miles on dried-up tank trails for physical fitness training, which resulted in sprained ankles and other injuries as well.

In the days I spent there, I could not wait to get away from the Tank Battalion, and fortunately, I was assigned to attend Advance Warehousing School back at Camp Lejeune of all places.

I was 23 years old when I was assigned to attend Advance Warehousing School. I requested to drive my own vehicle, a new Toyota Celica, to Camp Lejeune, and it got approved. And so, I drove my car all the way to the East Coast from San Diego.

During the trip to Camp Lejeune, I drove through my neighborhood in E. St. Louis and stopped to spend time with my parents as I hadn't seen them in years. By that time, most of my friends had either left for college or military service. Out of all my friends, only Blue, Reggie, and Buddy were left back in E. St. Louis.

Bridgette was there, too, living mostly in the streets near Washington Park. One of Bridgette's older sisters, Tracy Slack, was now giving me updates on Bridgette because she knew how I felt about her sister. The last time I received a call from Tracy was to inform me that they found Bridgette unresponsive outside of the Rail Road yard and thought that she was not going to make it. But she was now recovering in a substance abuse facility. I asked for the telephone number, and Tracy gave me the number, so I called Bridgette.

I asked Bridgette, "Do you remember me?"

She replied, "Of course I remember my friend!"

"I wanted you to know that you are loved, and I will always love you," I told her.

She responded, "I love you too."

"Bridgette, do you know what I miss the most about our childhood?" I asked her.

"What?" She asked curiously.

I responded with, "Our innocence."

That was the last time I talked to Bridgette. Years later, Blue called me to tell me that Bridgette was shot to death in Washington Park. I remember not crying this time, but I was somewhat relieved that Bridgette was no longer suffering.

"Black women are the most undervalued demographic in this country." In 2022 alone, more than 97,000 Black women were reported missing, according to the 2022 NCIC Missing Person and Unidentified Person Statistics.

Anyway, I did not stay there for long and continued my journey to Advance Warehousing School at Camp Lejeune.

After coming back to Camp Lejeune, I realized that it had not changed at all. I kept being pulled over by either the Military Police, Local Police, or the North Carolina State

Police just because I had Guam License plates and I was black.

I remember one weekend when I was driving on the roads of Wilmington, NC, and got pulled over. They gave me a ticket for speeding and fined me $75, which I had to pay on the spot; it was either that or going to jail.

I didn't have that kind of money on me at the time, so my fellow marines who were with me managed to gather the $75 so we could stay out of trouble and continue with our weekend.

Unfortunately, I had to show up at the Traffic Court the day before I graduated from Advance Warehousing School based on the charges of driving at an excessive speed. So, I got excused the day before graduation to attend Traffic Court.

The judge was stern and handed down punishments quickly before moving on to the next case. He suspended my driving license for one year.

I was not going to give up that easily, so I requested to talk to the judge and explained to him that I was not from North Carolina. I informed him that my family and I were stationed in California and that if my license was suspended for a year, I would have no way of getting my car back to California, where my family needed the vehicle.

The judge gave me a cold look and told me to go stand by the Court Police. After hearing two more cases, the judge called over the Court Police and said something to them. When they came back, they said, "It must be your lucky day because the judge gave you a fine instead of suspending your license." So, I was free to go after paying the fine.

But, to be honest, I was speeding about seven mph over the speed limit. Anyhow, I graduated the next day and left for San Diego and vowed never to come back to North Carolina again.

On my way back to San Diego, I once again stopped in E. St. Louis to visit my friends and family. I spent some time with my friends and spoke to Buddy about whether he had any plans of leaving. But, like his sister, he said he had no such plans.

I called my wife and asked her if she was okay with me bringing a friend back home so he could get a fresh start. She agreed, and I asked Buddy again if he was willing to leave after what had happened to his sister in E. St. Louis and come live with me in California.

Before he could say anything, his other two sisters answered for him. They said, "Yes, Buddy would love to go to California with you." Buddy also nodded to that and agreed to come with me.

And so, after a couple of days, Buddy and I left for California. A few days passed, and everything was going well; Buddy even got a job at the local Target Store and was saving up to get his own place.

Unfortunately, in the end, we cannot control our luck, good or bad. His good luck remained for a few days, and within a couple of months, he started spending time in the city with some of his old friends from E. St. Louis. Shortly after, Buddy moved out of my apartment to live with his friends from E. St. Louis. To make a long story short, within a couple of months of moving out, he was back in E. St. Louis.

As for me, my happiness only lasted for six weeks. I was back in the 1st Tank Battalion and had had enough of that place, so I thought about applying for Recruiting Duty or Drill Instructor. My wife did not agree with me on this decision but at least Drill Instructor Duty would be at MCRD, which was the same station as her. So, to get away from the 1st Tank Battalion, I applied for both positions. Within a month, I received orders to report to Drill Instructor School, MCRD, San Diego.

Before reporting to DI School, I took some time off to get back in shape and reported there in September 1986. The DI School was like Boot Camp but on steroids. To this day, Marine Corps Drill Instructor School is the toughest, most stressful, and most demanding school that I have ever attended.

It was extremely demanding work. In order to be a Drill Instructor, I got very little sleep and was required to be in excellent physical shape while serving as an example for the recruits.

In my opinion, Drill Instructor School was as difficult as Navy Seal Training, putting aside the swimming requirement. I remember that half of my fellow marines were dropped from the class before graduating.

There was a psyche exam as well, and if they saw any red flags, they failed the individual. If a DI School student could not keep up with the physical requirements, they would fail you, and if you could not verbally repeat every Drill Movement in the Marine Corps Drill Manual before graduation, they would drop you.

Before graduating from DI School, we had to complete a peer evaluation. If a DI School student was in the bottom 10% of the peer evaluation, then they would be dropped.

Before the exam day, we ran miles and performed other fitness training, staying up all night studying the drill manual. I enjoyed the Drill Instructor School, like my first boot camp from E. St. Louis. However, my being happy at school made some of my peers think I was overconfident.

The school was grueling, so I started spending more time on base studying, working out, drilling, and doing whatever I could to keep up with DI School, which also took a toll on my marriage. If I'm honest, things weren't the same after I came back from Advance Warehousing School, and I felt the growing distance between my wife and me.

While in DI school, my wife and I started talking about our marriage and whether we thought it was going to survive. I did not want to go through the misery that happened in Okinawa when I doubted her loyalty. Although I, too, was considering getting a divorce, if DI School found out I was going through a divorce while attending school, they would have discharged me immediately. Therefore, I kept it to myself, and we remained married.

In December 1986, I graduated from the Drill Instructor School. My wife and our daughter attended the ceremony. I remember when my daughter saw me in the drill instructor cover (hat) for the first time, she got scared and started crying. Being a father, I understood why she was crying, so I immediately took it off, and she stopped crying.

After I graduated from the Drill Instructor School, I was assigned to the 3rd Recruit Training Battalion, Lima Company, for Drill Instructor Duty.

People used to say that the DI cover has effects on people, and I was soon to find out. When I checked in to the 3rd Recruit Training Battalion, Lima Company, I got assigned to a three-man team. We were only three drill instructors, Sgt. Muniz, Senior Drill Instructor Sgt. Yerardi, and me, Sgt. Cason, assigned to train the entire platoon, so we used to rotate duty days every three days. On our duty days, we were required to sleep in the duty hut.

Senior Drill Instructor Yerardi was a disciplinarian and loved to punish recruits whenever he got the chance. Sgt. Muniz was the same way, and he and Sgt. Yerardi worked well together. So, I had to learn fast and keep up with Sgt. Yerardi's style of training.

Sgt. Muniz, who was training me as a new "green" junior Drill Instructor, remained patient with me, allowing me to find my ground, which I did. I caught on quickly and fell right in line with the team. I must say that after that first platoon, I became a little arrogant. That was unusual for young Drill Instructors, but being around Sgt. Muniz and Senior DI Yerardi, I was all in and couldn't wait until we picked up our new platoon.

Around that time, the Battalion Commanding Officer of the 3rd Recruit Training Battalion requested that I come to his office. I remember the exact words I thought after being summoned by the commanding officer, "Oh, shit, now what did I do to be called to the Battalion Commander's office?"

Once I got there, the Battalion Commander LtCol. Armbrister, who happened to be African American, asked me to come inside and tell him about my 1st Class Swimming classification. He further asked me if I had ever been assigned as a lifeguard and I informed him that I had, but that I did not get time to fulfill my duties.

LtCol. Armbrister then explained the reason he had called me to his office was that some of the black recruits were having a difficult time passing the swimming qualification in recruit training, and he wanted me to teach them. He also said that he thought placing a black swim instructor at the swim tank could help the black recruits pass the swim qualification and told me that he intended to send me to the swim tank as a swim instructor.

Being in shock, I laughed out loud. "What's funny about it?" he asked, raising his eyebrow, and I replied, "Nothing was funny, Sir." He then asked me what I thought about his idea, and I replied, "With all due respect, Sir, I did not come to Drill Instructor duty to teach recruits how to swim; I came to Drill Instructor duty to train recruits, Sir."

However, he did not really care about what I thought and informed me that I would be assigned to the swim tank. Although I tried to explain to him that I did not want to be a swim tank instructor, he did not listen, and I was dismissed.

I came back to the Lima Company disappointed and told everyone about my misery, but they all laughed at me and said that they wished they had the same opportunity as me. However, my feelings of disappointment remained the same.

A week later, I was instructed to report to the swim tank to take the test to become a swim instructor, and I did. However, I failed the test intentionally, making a mockery of the test, which made the Battalion Commander Officer livid, and I heard that he was out to even the score with me. But I paid it no mind and went back into the trenches, training recruits.

After a few cycles of drilling, I was already confident enough, eyeing the position of Senior Drill Instructor. As I was busy making my career, my married life was falling apart. My wife and I were contemplating divorce and discussing the custody of our daughter.

Since we were considering a divorce, there was no reason for us to stay together anymore, so I moved out of the apartment and started living on the Depot.

Drill Instructor duty was much more brutal than I initially thought it would be. I was on duty 18 hours a day and every third day, being on a three-man team, I had to do 24 hours a day and sleep in the duty hut. I spent 90% of my time on the base, fulfilling my duties, and the distance grew between me and my wife so we both agreed that we should go ahead with the divorce.

And so, in June 1987, we filed for divorce in Downtown San Diego, which cost us a total of $160, the amount we split. It only amounted to $160 as we got a military attorney on the base to draw up the divorce papers, and so we only had to pay the court filing fee and nothing else. We agreed on everything when it came to the little property we had and the child support.

The following month, in July 1987, things got really bad for me. A recruit falsely accused me of verbally and physically abusing him. However, it was not unusual for drill instructors to have allegations against them as recruits mostly made up things to get out of boot camp.

The recruit in question had tried everything he could to get discharged from the marines; in his arsenal of ways out was also a botched suicide attempt. So, I wasn't really worried about the allegations levied against me.

Perhaps I shouldn't have taken the whole matter so lightly because the next thing I knew, I was called to the Battalion Commander's Office, where they suspended me until further notification till the investigation was over. I admit that I was a bit nervous at the time because I was a man who had never been suspended before. But, at the same time, I was confident that they would not find a single piece of evidence of physical abuse against me, and I was sure that I would be back to work in no time.

In the middle of the investigation, I was assigned to the rifle range for annual qualification. I found it strange and thought to myself, '*Shouldn't I be there for the investigation?*' However, a week passed by, and they called me back to MCRD San Diego.

Unfortunately, as soon as I got back to MCRD, allegations were brought forward against me for verbally and physically abusing not just one but three recruits. I was terrified now and thought about what happened at MCRD when I was sent to Camp Pendleton for rifle qualification.

Terrified of being falsely accused and losing my career because of it, I asked the Company's 1st Sgt. Zamora what was going on, and he recommended that I get an attorney because the Battalion Commander, LtCol. Armbrister, was intent on getting me out and proving a point of disobeying his direct order to become a swimming instructor.

Although I did not want to believe someone could be so petty, soon after, I was notified that I had to appear in front of the Battalion Commander for Non-Judicial Punishment on July 22, 1987, just weeks after the initial allegation. This was unbelievable for me; '*how can someone be so brutal about such a little thing? Why are some people so cruel to others? Why do some people enjoy hurting others just because they did not do what they wanted?*' Those thoughts were running through my head as I wondered what was next for me.

Chapter 13: Humiliation, Suicide Thoughts, and Perseverance

Standing in front of the 3rd Battalion Commanding Officer, LtCol. Armbrister, I was ready to receive Non-Judicial Punishment (NJP) for the accusations of physical and verbal recruit abuse levied against me.

My Company Commander, Capt. Baker, Series Commander Lt. Williams, Company 1stSgt. Zamora, Sgt. Muniz, Sgt. Newsom, along with eight recruits, stood in the hallway on my behalf, ready to say that the allegations were false.

LtCol. Armbrister was getting agitated as the witnesses testified on my behalf, so he asked the witnesses to leave the office. After we re-entered his office, one of the eight recruits came forward first, claiming he was there at the drill. He said that he did not witness any physical abuse and that it was a false accusation. Hearing this, LtCol. Armbrister asked if the rest of the seven were going to give the same statement.

The 1st Sgt Zamora said, " I don't know, but I believe that to be true, and all the recruits will be witnesses for Drill Instructor Sgt. Cason."

The next recruit called in was the one who had initially accused me of abusing him physically and verbally.

Surprisingly, he took a 180-turn and gave a statement in my favor, mentioning that the initial statement he made regarding the abuse was false and that he was confused during the questioning.

After hearing his statement, LtCol. Armbrister decided he had heard enough and said he didn't want to hear more statements from the witnesses. Next, he asked for my statement. I stood by my initial statement and said that I was not guilty of any of the allegations brought against me and that I had never abused any recruit in any capacity whatsoever. When I was done with my statement, LtCol. Armbrister stated that he found me guilty.

Surprised by his verdict, I blurted out that I wanted a court-martial, the military's highest-level trial court. LtCol. Armbrister informed me that it was too late to request a court-martial, but with luck on my side, the 1st Sgt. interrupted LtCol. Saying, "He is indeed in his rights to request a court-martial."

LtCol. Armbrister asked his legal counsel, who was present in his office at the time, and they took the decision in my favor, saying, "Sgt. Cason has the right to request a court-martial before the findings of guilt/innocence and or before the punishment has been imposed."

LtCol. Armbrister then calmly said to me that he did not understand why I would request a court-martial since the charges were minor and that I had done a great job as a Drill

Instructor since joining his Battalion. He further added that he may find me innocent of all charges and send me back to work.

"Do you really need to request a court-martial, or would you accept the NJP proceeding?" he reconfirmed.

Hearing his calm voice, I fell into the trap and agreed to continue with the NJP proceeding. As soon as I said that I would go with the NJP, LtCol. Armbrister raised his voice and said that he found me guilty and reduced my rank to CPL, immediately relieving me from Drill Instructor duty.

The whole office went silent; this was unexpected for me and for everyone else in attendance. Finally, I gathered my senses and asked LtCol. Armbrister if I could speak to which he said, "That is all and you are dismissed."

I proceeded to speak anyway to clarify my position, but he cut me off and dismissed me. Still in a state of shock and disbelief about what had just transpired, I walked outside the office, slamming the door behind me.

As I was walking away, I heard LtCol. Armbrister yell for me to get back in the office. Then, someone inside the office opened the door while he ordered me to get back in.

As I reentered the office, I stood in front of LtCol. Armbrister's desk, and he yelled again, "Now you are dismissed. Leave properly." I replied, "Yes, Sir!" and did the exact same thing again, slamming the door even harder this time. I could hear him shouting at everyone to leave his office as I was walking outside the building. I could almost imagine him turning red with rage, but I couldn't care less at the time – my whole life had been shaken because of something I didn't even do.

I thought I was doing great, even moving up the ladder in my career. I thought I would get out of it, but a wave of devastating accusations flipped the coin. It was a blow to my career. I was devastated while both Sergeants, my Company Commander, Series Commander, and Company 1stSgt. tried to console me, but when they said they had never experienced such NJP, it just made me frustrated.

The 1st Sgt suggested I should start the appeal process immediately, and I still remember telling him, "You know that the appeal process is bullshit," and walking out of there and heading to the Recruit Regiment Headquarters.

Once I got there, I went to the Recruit Regiment SgtMaj's office to speak with SgtMaj Overstreet directly. As I walked directly into his office, SgtMaj Overstreet was shocked. However, I explained the whole situation to him and asked him how he could help me in the matter. To my dismay, he suggested the same thing as the 1st Sgt. had suggested: requesting an appeal and letting the process take its course.

I started feeling anxious due to the fear of failure. I felt as if I was all alone and asked myself what had just happened. This was the worst day of my life, and there was nothing I could do about it. Still in a state of shock and disbelief, I went into my room and cried my heart out. I was embarrassed, scared, disappointed, and betrayed as I was in devastating emotional pain. I had nowhere to turn, so I started drinking until I passed out. All I can remember is that when I came to, nothing had changed, so I continued drinking until I passed out again.

I was already going through a lot in my personal life at the time with the divorce and losing primary custody of my little girl. So, this seemed like the nail in the coffin for me. I had hit rock bottom and had no hope left for a bright future.

Two days passed with me drowning my sorrows in the bottle and not leaving my room. Eventually, I started looking for pills that could save me from misery. Something that would end it all. I was feeling overwhelmed, hopeless, and unsure where to turn for support; I wanted to take my own life. I could not even imagine starting over as a CPL and facing the Drill Instructors who were on my team; my embarrassment had reached its peak.

Unable to find any pills, I went to the liquor store, thinking that I could drink myself to death. I bought the liquor, went back home, and drank to the extent that I passed out again. For four days, drinking and passing out remained the routine. I did not shave, I did not take a shower or change clothes, and I did not leave my room.

On the fifth day, I opened my eyes when I heard someone pounding on my door. I didn't want to get up or meet anyone, so I let it be. However, when the intensity of the pounding increased, I shouted, "Go away!" after which I heard, "Open the got damn door." I recognized the voice; it was the Company 1st Sgt. so I opened the door.

As soon as I opened the door, he could see the misery my life had become; he was shocked watching the room and my condition. I remember him asking what the hell I was doing and me replying, "Minding my own business."

The 1st Sgt. got irritated and said, "You need to get your head out of your ass and get dressed before they charge you with Unauthorized Absence (UA)."

I remember asking, "What are they going to do? Bust me again? Like I give a damn," adding to his anger and irritation. He told me he did not believe I could be a quitter and that I only had a few days to submit an appeal. He further said that he truly believed that my appeal would be overturned.

He gave me the motivation and purpose to fight. I got up, took a shower, and got dressed. However, I was not in my Sgt. stripes, so I asked him if there would be any problem with not being in my uniform. He told me that I could correct that later, but for the time being, I had to submit my appeal. So, that's what I did; I went to the legal counsel and submitted my intent to appeal.

What happened next was just as painful and even worse than the NJP as I was ostracized by the drill instructors in my Company. They did not even look me in the eye and dismissed the matter, not wanting to get involved. They were the people I considered my friends, but the friendship suddenly disappeared as they did not support me, and I felt as if I was on an island and everyone had deserted me.

I was heartbroken, but how can anyone who hasn't experienced what I did understand the pain as intense as any open-heart surgery without anesthesia, with no cuts or bruises to show? How can anyone who hasn't experienced what I did understand the complexity of pain that is unbearably intense? How can anyone who hasn't experienced what I did understand the embarrassment and failure that I was drowning in?

I was lost, stuck, and devastated in the unending maze of destruction, so I had to do some soul-searching to figure out my purpose, my motivation, and how I could change my life by aiming for all that I needed.

I can still recall how difficult it was for me to call my parents and inform them of what I had been through. Like any parent, they were disappointed, especially my stepfather, but they were both supportive of me. I remember them telling me to hang in there, keep my head up, and that they would be praying for me.

I began to pray for answers from God. "Why me?" I asked him. "What was I supposed to learn from this? Is this beneficial for me somehow?" I prayed to God and asked for His help, as He was the only one who could guide me through this tough time. I was just breathing at the time, not dead, not alive, just breathing.

I took it one step at a time, but the strange thing was, my whole life was surrounded by the rank of Sergeant and Drill Instructor, and that was what I became, the Drill Instructor Sgt. Cason. I thought about who I was and what I was without the title and the rank; I was lost, but the only choice I had at the time was to keep breathing.

Walking across the Depot to the tailor holding my uniform tops to replace the Sgt stripes with the CPL stripes, I can still recall the embarrassment as the other DIs were pointing at me like I was some kind of plague.

I was devastated, but as soon as I wore the uniform with the LCpl stripes, somehow, I realized that I was the same person and that the stripes or the rank did not define me. I realized that I might have been knocked down, but I was still the same Cedric from E. St. Louis who never gave up on his dreams, and no obstacle could stop him from getting what he wanted.

That experience gave me the confidence and motivation to start with my appeal, and I waited anxiously for the decision from the Regiment Commanding Officer.

I would be remiss if I did not mention the only two Drill Instructors who supported me and kept me uplifted and busy during a tough time in my life. They were Sgt. Muniz and Sgt. Chesky. Sgt. Muniz was on my very first team and we had become friends. As a matter of fact, I served as Best Man at Sgt. Muniz's wedding. As for Sgt. Chesky, he would come by my room, and we used to hang out on his boat on weekends and in Palm Springs for spring break with his girlfriend and her friends.

About a month later, on August 20, 1987, my appeal was denied by the Commanding Officer of the Recruit Training Regimen. I was shaken by this decision; I could not believe that my appeal was denied even though it was submitted with all the witnesses' statements.

How could he deny my appeal when everyone knew that I was railroaded? How could he not see the truth? How could he not give me justice? My mind was reeling.

The denied appeal stated that it would be forwarded to the Marine Corps Recruit Depot (MCRD) Commanding General for his review and decision. By that time, I just knew that this was just protocol, so I was not expecting my appeal to suddenly be overturned.

On top of denying my appeal, they gave me one more punishment the day after the decision came. I received temporary orders to report to San Diego, Naval Station 32nd St. I was assigned to Navy Shore Patrol duty for sixty days. This left me wondering who else I had made angry.

However, I reported to Naval Station 32nd St., Shore Patrol School for training, and after a couple of days of training, I was stationed on shore patrol. My duty included picking up drunken sailors and marines every morning at the border across from Tijuana, Mexico.

I remember one day, most of the drunken sailors and marines were arrested the night before by the Mexicali Police, robbed of all of their money, and beaten up. When I spoke to them, most of them reported that it was the police that robbed and beat them, and I kept wondering why they kept going over the border after facing such humiliation.

Another reason I hated the shore patrol duty was patrolling off-base military housing. This duty also made me sad as most of the time, I had to stop the sailors, coming back home from a six-month tour, from hurting their cheating wives. Some of them even came home to find another man living in their home.

While on Shore Patrol, I received my appeal results from the Marine Corps Recruit Depot Commanding General. Opening the documents, a glimmer of hope returned in me, and I thought that it would get accepted this time, but, lo and behold, it was denied again.

After my 60 days of Shore Patrol duty were up, I reported back to MCRD 3rd Battalion, where I was notified that I was getting reassigned from the Recruit Regiment to the Headquarters and Service Battalion. The only thought that came to my mind at the time was, "Wow, now I get to work on the base where everyone knows me, and I am still a CPL." The only silver lining that I could see about being at the MCRD San Diego was that I got to see my daughter as she was attending daycare on the Depot.

Reporting back to the Headquarters and Service Battalion, I found out that I was assigned to the Purchasing and Contracting Department. I remember saying to myself, "Wow, of all places, why was I assigned to Purchasing and Contracting? I have no experience in Government Purchasing and Contracting."

The Battalion Contracting Officer, Capt. Hepburn, was very generous and did not prejudge me. He gave me the opportunity to go toward success like anyone else in the Purchasing Department. Even though he gave me one of the toughest assignments within the department, the Follow-up Desk, I was sure that he did not mean any harm.

This desk was the only one in the department that was stacked with outdated Contracts and Overdue Open Orders that had been opened for years with no clear way to complete or close. Capt. Hepburn clearly took me as a person who could do the job in the best possible way.

With no experience in Government Procurement, I was confused about everything. But I learned quickly that no one really cared about how the government spent its money, and it was not a priority if they got what they were paid for. Hence, the desk was overflowing with old open contracts, and a ton of overdue open orders were given to me.

As I was a very organized person from the start, I started filing contacts and orders by their dates and due dates. Once I got everything organized, I started reviewing the contracts and orders and contacting people. I realized that no one had ever followed up on the contacts and orders. So, shortly after contacting companies and contractors, things started to be delivered, and I was able to close out overdue orders and complete contracts.

Even though some of the contractors and vendors were difficult to deal with, I did not give up and started calling them again with a different voice, pretending that I was from a law firm representing the government, following up on overdue contracts and open orders that had yet to be fulfilled. It was just a matter of a few days before things started clearing up quickly. So quick, in fact, that within the first six months, 90% of the work on my desk was cleared.

Capt. Hepburn was astonished. He wanted me to consider changing my MOS to 3044 Purchasing and Contracting Specialist. Fortunately, things were finally going well, so I reached out to my wife to see if we could try to reconcile. A relationship involves both people who are willing to work things out and make sacrifices for each other. But that is not always the reality, especially if your partner believes that the marriage is not worth saving. No one can save a marriage with a one-sided effort.

My wife informed me that she knew about my demotion and all the things I had been through. She further said that she had already moved on from me. I knew that rebuilding a relationship takes time; marriage is a partnership, a friendship enveloped in love and compassion where both spouses compromise. But if one of them is unwilling to reconcile and refuses on the spot, then nothing much is left to work on as it takes two people to reconcile. This was the last time for me, and I vowed to myself at that time that I would never get married again.

Our divorce was finalized on December 17, 1987. I remember hanging the divorce papers on the board next to my desk as a celebration of being free once again and as a reminder to never get married again.

You cannot really know how something feels without experiencing it yourself. I experienced marriage and understood it on a personal level. Any divorced person can understand the feeling and agree with that. I was fully qualified to judge that I did not find it suitable for my future after experiencing a marriage. I simply did not!

Chapter 14: On-going, a Son, and Hope

As a Purchasing and Contracting Specialist, things were finally starting to settle down, and I genuinely enjoyed my position. My divorce had been finalized, and I could put my past behind me and spend quality time with my daughter.

A few years ago, getting married and having children were at the top of my goals, but considering the events of the last two years, those goals shifted, and marrying again was off my list. Although I stepped back into the dating scene soon after, I did not want to marry ever again. So, I was honest and upfront with whoever I dated.

Soon after the divorce, I met an attractive young woman from Mississippi who had come to visit her brother, a marine stationed on MCRD. Considering her beauty, she was popular on the base, so I asked her out on a date, and we went out a couple of times.

After going on several dates, a man approached me and claimed that she was his woman, so I backed off. However, she never acted like she was involved with anyone, so I went on a date with her again. After that date, the same man started telling everyone that I was trying to break their relationship.

Tired of the rumors, I went up to him and told him that if he had a problem with me, he should talk to the girl he claimed to be hers about it. But he never did, and we started seeing each other on a regular basis off-base to avoid the drama.

As things started to get serious with her, I reminded myself and also told her that I had no plans of getting married or having any more children. Surprisingly, she had no problem with my perspective and understood why I was not looking into settling down. As a matter of fact, she was not interested in getting married either, as she could not have children.

Time went on, and we started to spend more time with each other. As we both had roommates, we decided to get a separate apartment and move in together.

My life was going well, both personal and professional, and then one day, Capt. Hepburn came to me and asked, "Who did you piss off this time?" Not sure what he was talking about or what had happened, I replied, "No one that I know of, why?" He then notified me that I had orders to the Non-Commissioned Officer (NCO) Leadership School. This was a school for young Corporals and Sergeants to help them grow in their leadership skills, such as Drill, Physical Fitness, Marine Corps Traditions, and Field Training.

As a prior Drill Instructor, this was like sending an Eagle Scout to join the Cub Scouts. I could not believe that someone was still out there trying to punish me by embarrassing me. But indeed, there was someone, because when I asked our Headquarters and Service Battalion SgtMaj, he informed me that someone from the Depot Headquarters had recommended that I get sent to NCO School.

Despite being on the verge of exploding with embarrassment, I reported to NCO Leadership School located on MCRD San Diego, CA, on February 7, 1988.

The NCO School instructors had probably heard that I was a prior drill instructor because it seemed like they were out to get me, as the harassment started on day one. They were radiating the vibes like they were saying, "Who does he think he is?" But I remained quiet and humble even when I knew they were teaching drill incorrectly.

None of the NOC Instructors were prior Drill Instructors, and I could tell my Platoon Instructor was a little intimidated by me, but at least he was wise enough to ask me to teach drills to our platoon. I taught drills, and we ended up winning the Drill Competition in the class.

As a prior Drill Instructor, NCO School was amusing. It was more like a small vacation for me, and I really enjoyed helping my fellow NCO classmates. They all looked up to me for guidance, and I was happy to assist them regardless of what platoon they were assigned to.

When it was time for the final examination, I was confident that I was going to ace the drill exercise. However, one of the instructors, Sgt. Reaves, gave me a less than 100% grade, which made me upset, and I went to ask him about the grading. I remember him saying, "I don't believe in perfect scores," and walking away as I stood there, mouth hanging wide open, thinking, "Really? Whatever!"

Seeing my performance and up-to-the-mark drills, everyone thought that I would graduate as the top student. As a top student, I would be number one, which meant I would have averaged the top scores or grades across the board, including the highest score in Physical Fitness. However, I should have known better than to hope for something I rightfully deserved, considering how life had been treating me recently.

A few days before graduation, the chief instructor, GySgt Mitchell, requested I report to his office. When I reported to his office, he informed me that I was not graduating at the top of the class as an Honor Student. Shocked and in a state of disbelief, I asked, "Why not?"

He answered my question calmly and said that he had received a call from MCRD Headquarters (Commanding General's Office) and had been instructed that I could not graduate as an honor student from NCO school. Not only that but he was also instructed that a white female marine would graduate as the honor student; she had scored high on the final academic exam. GySgt Mitchell apologized to me as well, and that was when I knew that he had nothing to do with it.

During the graduation ceremony, while awards were being presented, GySgt Mitchell called me to the podium and started announcing my awards; Physical Fitness Achievement Award for a perfect score of 300, Military Excellence Award for Academics High Score, Certificate of Excellence and Leadership from the NCO Association, and then the icing on the cake was the Leadership Award, which entails being presented a plaque with a real USMC K-Bar attached in honor of the top Leader of the Class.

As I received all the awards, I could hear everyone applauding and cheering for me, and they kept applauding until I came back to my seat and sat down.

Then, GySgt Mitchell called for the class Honor Student to come to the podium. The award she received was an Award for Academics and nothing else. As people waited for more, GySgt Mitchell announced to the audience that it was the end of the ceremony while he kept looking at me.

Everyone started whispering, asking how she got to be the honor student. I, on the other hand, felt bad for her and wished that she hadn't been put in that position. However,

I believe that GySgt Mitchell wanted to make a statement and show everyone how unfair it was that he was instructed to make someone else the Honor Student.

When I came back to the Purchasing and Contracting department after NCO school, I started where I left off and cleaned up all the old and overdue contacts. As soon as I was back, Capt. Hepburn recommended I attend Purchasing and Contracting Small Purchase Defense School at the Naval Station, San Diego, CA. So, I went there and graduated on May 6, 1988.

After my graduation, Capt. Hepburn put in a request for my MOS to be changed from warehouse supply clerk to Purchasing and Contraction Specialist. However, because of my prior NJP on the drill field, his request was denied. Still, Capt. Hepburn did not lose hope, and he placed me up for the Depot Marine NCO of the Quarter. But that, too, got denied at the Depot Headquarters level, and I could not even be interviewed for consideration. It had been a year, and I was still getting punished for the accusations that got me into this mess.

During that time, my live-in relationship partner started getting serious about our relationship and asked me to get married. However, I backed off and told her that my mind had never changed, and I was still adamant about not marrying again for the rest of my life. However, she either chose not to listen or believed that I would change my mind because she kept bringing up the topic of marriage in every one of our conversations. I had to draw the line as I did not want her to get her hopes high. I told her, "Maybe we should consider getting our own places."

Naturally, she was very upset and hurt and could not believe that I was serious. However, I was just not ready to even think about getting married again after my divorce. Therefore, I was okay with shacking even though I knew it would hurt her in the long run. I just wanted my cake and wanted to eat it, too, to be honest.

However, in order to avoid any miscommunication, the next time the marriage thing came up, I told her that I would move out and that we could still be friends.

Finally realizing that I would never marry her, she was devastated. However, I went on ahead and placed my letter in the apartment office, notifying them that I would be moving out in 30 days.

As I told her about my moving out, she gave me the news, which blew up my mind; she was pregnant. Saying that I was shocked would be an understatement. I could not accept the fact that she was carrying my child because, at the start of our relationship, she had informed me that she could not get pregnant.

In a state of shock, I kept asking her, "What do you want to do now?" and she kept saying that she was keeping her baby. But I was not asking about the baby; I was asking about the apartment, so I said, "I meant about the apartment because I am still moving out."

She was infuriated, and I knew what I was doing was hurting her, but I had never lied to her, and that helped me move forward in the next stage of my life. So, after a month, I moved out as planned. I found an apartment with a new roommate, a marine working in the same building that I was on MCRD as a Supply Clerk. We found an apartment in the same complex that I was currently living in.

When I moved out of the apartment, she moved in with her sister, who came over from Mississippi. After we separated, we did not see each other much and tried to keep our distance.

One evening, I went on a date, and she saw me. It was natural for her to be angry as she was still pregnant with my child and I was dating other women. Even though I felt awful, I was still convinced that I was never going to get married again.

I took full responsibility for hurting her and vowed never to get serious with anyone again, especially to the point of moving in with them. But it was too late for her. She was shattered after getting abandoned by the person she thought she would marry.

I remember my new roommate asking me, "How could you be so cold and inconsiderate of her feelings?" and I asked him, "What should I do, get married only to get divorced in a couple of years?" I also informed him of the fact that I never lied to her; she knew from the start I had no intentions of marrying anyone.

***

My 1stSgt from Lima Company was transferred to Headquarters and Service Battalion, H&S Company, where I was currently working. One day, 1stSgt. Zamora asked me about my appeal, and I informed him about how they were getting rejected and denied. He was disappointed and told me that I should get a civilian lawyer. However, I could not afford a civilian lawyer on a Cpl. salary with child support payments. So, 1stSgt. Zamora informed me about a lawyer off base who did pro bono cases for Marine Drill Instructors. Moreover, she did not ask for payment unless she won the case. Hearing this, my hopes got lifted, so I took her contact information from the 1stSgt.

Next week, I contacted the lawyer, Alice Cate. After hearing my problem, she could not believe my story and that something terrible like this could happen to someone. So, she immediately took my case and informed me that we would submit an appeal to the secretary of the Navy, Board of Corrections.

On November 8, 1988, I submitted my appeal to the secretary of the Navy on the basis of error and injustice. On February 23, 1989, I received a letter sent from the Commandant of the Marine Corps (CMC) to the Secretary of the Navy, Board of Corrections. The letter stated, "No legal basis for relief was found. Therefore, this additional appeal will be denied."

I was ready to give up then, but Alice informed me that she expected this and that we would submit a rebuttal to the CMC response.

A few months went by, and on March 21, 1989, my son was born at Sharp Memorial Hospital in San Diego, CA. I received a call from my ex-girlfriend's sister to inform me about the birth of my son. I was upset I was not there at the time of his birth and asked her why she had not called me before. She then informed me that her older sister did not believe that I deserved to be there when he was born. Anyhow, I visited my son in the hospital.

My rebuttal to the secretary of the navy was submitted on March 28, 1989, by Alice on my behalf, challenging the basis of the Commandant of the Marine Corps decision.

As I waited for the response from the Secretary, I was promoted to my previous position as Sergeant on my own merit on April 1, 1989. I was on cloud nine as I was promoted back to Sergeant, so I went to the tailor and asked him to put back my Sergeant stripes on my uniform.

I was relieved being in my previous position as I had to support two children now, a daughter and a son. After I got promoted, I received a post about the opening of an instructor job at NCO School, so I immediately applied for the position even though I believed I would never be considered as the instructor due to my history.

However, about a month later, I was notified that I had an interview for the instructor position. Getting the news, I was blown away that I was even considered and thought that it must be GySgt. Mitchell, who had recommended me.

However, I found out that GySgt. Mitchell was relieved and was replaced by the new Chief instructor at NCO School, who happened to be none other than GySgt. Colon, the previous Regimental Drill Master for Recruit Training Regiment (RTR), MCRD. He was well aware of my history as he was the RTR Drill Master when I got busted to Corporal.

GySgt. Colon was known all over the base for being extremely harsh on drill instructors because he graded all platoons and their drill instructors during drill evaluations. He had a nickname on base as "Darth Vader" because, with one swipe of his pin, he would send drill instructors to be placed on other duties, removing them from training recruits because they could not train recruits to drill.

Drill instructors used to be graded on their drill knowledge, and the scoring was from 0 to 10. The Drill

Instructors who scored lower than a seven were not considered drill instructors, and they would likely end up teaching Marine Corps history, Physical Fitness, Rifle Range, or at the Swim Tank only if the individual was a 1st Class swimmer. When I found out who was in charge, I knew there was no way in hell I would be selected as an instructor at NCO School.

When I reported to GySgt Colon for an interview, the first thing he did was inspect my uniform. He did not utter a single word and directly went to inspect my uniform with a ruler like I was a student at NCO School.

It was embarrassing for me, but I stood still until he was done with the inspection. After inspecting my uniform, GySgt Colon informed me that he knew about my history, the allegations, NJP, and the demotion. This was the only thing he said to me, and then he dismissed me. Leaving his office, I went back to work at the Purchasing and Contracting Department.

Chapter 15: Instructor Again, Redemption and Back to Okinawa

I was back to my old position in Purchasing and Contracting, dating someone new, and living with a roommate. I started dating multiple women and acting as if I would never get into a serious relationship again. Not only this, but I also introduced the women I was dating to each other and invited them to the pool parties that my roommate and I would host.

This was my way of not hurting anyone anymore; I thought if they were okay with me seeing other people, so be it, and if they were not, then so be it.

As I was being transparent with all the women I was dating, my roommate and other friends thought that I was a madman and started giving them nicknames based on their personalities. However, I was just being honest with the girls; I was not going to unintentionally mislead any women ever again and save myself the trouble if that were to happen.

Even though I was promoted back to Sergeant, I worked part-time at "J." Riggins Clothing Store in the Mission Valley Mall and at the Warehouse Record Store in Kearny Mesa. I worked hard to fulfill the child support for my daughter and son and also because I had a certain lifestyle that I wanted to maintain, and the Sergeant's paycheck wasn't cutting it for me.

Sometimes, I wonder whether I could have been a better father. The answer is always the same, "Absolutely!"

When I look back at the time, I think my roommate and I were both out of control as we were living as bachelors and pushed each other to the limit. Amidst all the partying and dating around, there was one girl whom I had feelings for, and I did not want to mess up the relationship I had with her. Thus, I intentionally kept her at a distance from my shenanigans.

However, our relationship started to get serious as we started to spend much of our time dating. Fortunately, she did not want to take things any further, so dating her was easy for me.

I was developing feelings for her, and I remember thinking that if I were to get serious with someone again, it would be her. Then, lo and behold, I caught her with another guy. But what could I do? I could not blame her as I was doing the same thing, but maybe it was my manhood that would not accept losing her to someone. So, I did not give up and fought to hold on to our relationship and won.

While I was getting into a serious relationship, dating the woman I felt was the one, my ex-wife notified me that she received orders to be stationed at Okinawa. She further informed me that she was not able to take our daughter with her. Hearing this, I suggested that I should take full custody of her, but she did not agree with me.

My ex-wife recommended that our daughter should stay with her mother in Wisconsin for a year until she returned to the US.

As I was still struggling because of the tragedies I had gone through, I was conflicted by the thought of not being able to see my daughter. Nevertheless, I approved my ex-wife's suggestion, and then it was decided that my daughter would live with her grandmother, and I would not be able to see her for a whole year.

I vividly remember the day my daughter had to leave for Wisconsin as I was having a change of mind about her living with her grandmother instead of me. But it was too late now, and I could do nothing but send her to her grandmother's.

Before she went to Wisconsin, I took her shopping, where I bought winter clothes and a winter coat, and when it was time to say goodbye, I bawled like a baby. Even before she went away, I was already missing her and said goodbye while crying.

Watching me cry and sob, she started to cry as well, but I stopped for her sake, gave her a big hug, told her that I would come to visit her in Wisconsin, and left.

Around May 1989, I got a call in which I was informed that I was selected as an Instructor at the Non-Commissioned Officer (NCO) Leadership School. I was ecstatic and blown away by this second chance and having another opportunity to achieve my goals and dreams.

As I had to leave my previous department, the Purchasing and Contracting Department, they threw me a great going away party and presented me with a plaque on May 25, 1989.

So, there I was, reporting to the NCO School as a Leadership Instructor. It was good to be back, to set things right, and to make choices that would lead me to a better future.

I vividly remember running into Sgt Reaves, the instructor who cheated me on the final drill evaluation. Surprisingly, the first thing he did after running into me was to apologize for the low grade and explain that it was not his call. I responded to him politely and said that I had figured that he had nothing to do with it, and we got along well after that.

After I had settled in, the chief instructor GySgt. Colon called me into his office and explained why he had selected me as an instructor. He said I was the best candidate for the position. He also said that he did not believe in past mistakes and expected nothing but excellence from me as an instructor at NCO School and for me to be the rabbit for all the timed runs.

As drill instructors, whoever was the best runner in the company was the rabbit to lead the pace during timed runs. So, I was also responsible for teaching all drill movements to the students.

As GySgt. Colon had the background of a drill master for RTR, I was both excited and grateful that he had confidence in me, deeming me perfect for the position. Before I left his office, he said something that I can never forget, "Let us teach them how to be leaders in our beloved Marine Corps, that's all." He was confident that I could bring change to the school, and his words have stayed with me to this day.

The NCO School instructors received me very well, and we made a great team. The people involved in the initial team were GySgt. Colon, the Chief Instructor, SSgt. Johnson was in the USMC History, Sgt. Whobrey was responsible for Physical Fitness and First Aid, Sgt. Reaves was in Field Infantry/Land Navigation, and I, Sgt. Cason, was responsible for Drills and Ceremonies.

We worked really hard in every class, as our schedules were extremely demanding and challenging. Each of the active-duty marine classes lasted four weeks, and each of the reserve-duty marines classes lasted ten days. We graduated from one class one day and picked up another class the next day to begin training all over again. Even though we beavered away during that time, this was the best duty I ever had while serving in the Marine Corps.

Being an instructor at the Non-Commissioned Officer Leadership School was the best thing that happened to me, and I loved doing that. Moreover, my platoons were the ones who almost always took most of the awards when it came to Drill, Physical Fitness, and Academics. I had never witnessed a marine beside me who was so dedicated to the Marine Corps until I worked with GySgt. Colon.

Just like my stepfather taught me what a father is, AJ taught me everything happens for a reason, GySgt. Hunt taught me everyone deserves a second chance, and then there was GySgt. Robert Charlie Colon who walked the walk and talked the talk on the Spirit of the United States Marine Corps. GySgt. Colon's loyalty and commitment to the Corps made me start loving the Marine Corps and feel proud to be part of this Brotherhood. However, despite all that, nothing could make me forget what the Corps did to me and my family; the dark, gloomy depths in my heart caused by them were never to be healed.

Soon after reporting to the NCO School as a leadership instructor, I received a letter from the Department of Secretary of the Navy, Chairman, Board of Corrections of Navy records stating, "The Non-Judicial Punishment (NJP) received on July 22, 1987, was given unfairly, was as error, and concluded with injustice finds."

I jumped with excitement after reading the letter, as it took almost two years, but justice did prevail. As my lawyer, Alice Cate, read the letter out loud to me, I was in a state of total shock. I could not believe it at first, but when Alice explained that we had won the appeal and my record was wiped clean, I realized that it was really happening.

Not only that, but the letter had orders directing the Commandant of the Marine Corps (CMC) to remove all records of the NJP, award back pay, reinstate Drill Instructor status, and be promoted as warranted as if the NJP had never happened.

I was in a nostalgic trance, remembering the hell I went through. I started to cry, thinking how I had suicidal thoughts and how humiliated I was when my rank was dropped to Cpl. in front of my peers. I started to wonder, what if my family was still intact? What if my little girl was still living with me? What if this did not happen to me; would I be living a happily married life? What if...

Thinking about all that made me upset and angry about all the tragedy I went through because of that one LtCol., who wanted to put me down and wanted to prove his point, and why? Just because I did not want to be a swimming instructor.

After getting the good news, I went back to the past and went into a bout of depression as I still could not believe that after everything I had gone through, the after-effects of the damage were still there. Although it had to come to an end, it wasn't going to fix the hurt and the pain that followed me for years. However, eventually, I realized that I had to live with that for the rest of my life.

I remember when Alice Cate handed over the letter to me, she said that I should frame it. However, the first thought that occurred to me after hearing her say that was that the last thing I wanted was to be reminded of the hell I went through. So, I said to her, "No, I will not frame this letter, nor will I tear it."

The next day, when I reported back to duty at NCO School, I requested a meeting with GySgt. Colon, as I could not wait to show that letter to him. When I entered GySgt. Colon's office, I handed him the letter from the Department of the Secretary of the Navy. As he read the letter, his face lit up with a big smile, and he said in a loud voice, "It is about goddamn time! Congratulations Sgt. Cason, and my apologies for you having to go through all of this just to get justice, but you did it, and now it is time to move on."

GySgt. Colon apologized to me on behalf of the Marine Corps, and he meant what he said. I asked him how soon all of these allegations could be pulled off me, and he asked me to be patient. He said, "Remember, the Marine Corps has a black eye now, and it will take some time for them to receive and activate what the Secretary of the Navy has directed them to do."

He further told me that it could take months before any of those things in the letter would happen, asked me to be patient as the worst was over now, and congratulated me again.

I took my leave and went to teach my first class of the day. As I completed my class, word had already gotten out that I had won my appeal. So, as soon as I left the class, Sgt. Tony Reaves was waiting to congratulate me; he was the first person to congratulate me after GySgt. Colon. Then, the rest of the instructors followed to do the same as everyone was excited and happy for me.

I called my parents with the news, and I remember them saying that they were pleased that all of my misery had come to an end. They praised God and thanked Him for answering their prayers.

Before I knew it, the news was all over the depot. When I went back to Purchasing and Contracting, they already knew about the news, and everyone in the department congratulated me on winning my appeal before I could say anything about it.

The following week, I had to report to Camp Pendleton to attend the Formal School Instructor Course, a requirement for all the instructors if they were an instructor at any formal school in the Marine Corps.

On June 30, 1989, I graduated from the Formal School Instructor Course. I was still living with my roommate. One morning, when my roommate walked into my room without knocking, I was with the girl I had been serious about for so long. Watching him enter our room, we both were startled, but he seemed like he had just come from a party and apologized for walking in without knocking.

However, this offended her, and she was pretty upset and uncomfortable about staying over, so she left. It was then that I realized that it was time for me to move out. Therefore, a couple of weeks later, I notified my roommate that I would move out in thirty days as I wanted to get my own place.

The news of my moving out shocked him, but eventually, he understood that it was important for me to move out. So, after a month, I moved to my new apartment, and Sgt. Reaves and Sgt. Whobrey helped me move to my new apartment on Louisiana Street located in North Park, San Diego, which was a lot closer to the Depot.

As I moved into the new apartment, my girlfriend at the time expected to move in with me but I refused and put an end to that immediately. I explained to her that I was not going to live with another woman unless we were married, and I didn't plan on ever getting married.

Although she was disappointed at the time, she understood and that was what was so special about her and made me attracted to her more. However, even after that conversation, just about every time I came back to my apartment, she would be in her car waiting for me to come home. At the time, I did not mind as I lived in North Park, which was close to where she lived.

After a couple of months, I received my back pay from the Marine Corps and everything started to go well in my life. However, I was still waiting for the Marine Corps to review my promotion status, as I had never been promoted. I thought I would have been promoted to the rank of Staff Sergeant, SSgt., by now if the NJP never happened.

It took until October 1989 for the Marine Corps to authorize me to submit a request for consideration for remedial promotion to SSgt. I received orders to report to the 3rd Marine Division, Okinawa, Japan, by April 15, 1990. After I received the orders, I got a call from Washington DC, Marine Corps Headquarters. They asked me where I wanted to be stationed after returning to the US from Okinawa.

I was stunned because the Marine Corps never asked anyone where they wanted to be stationed. I told them that I wanted to return to Drill Instructor duty back at MCRD San Diego. However, the person I was talking to thought I was crazy to want to go back to the Drill Field. So, I explained to him that the reason I wanted to go back was that I did not like the way I left the last time I was on the Drill Field.

He then informed me that he would approve of me going back to the Drill Instructor Duty after I returned from Okinawa.

In December 1989, I received a letter from the CMC approving the recommendation for my promotion to SSgt. and backdating the effective date to May 1, 1989.

I remember I returned home to E. St. Louis for Christmas to spend time with my parents and other family members. I rented a car, called my ex-wife's mother, and notified her of my intention to visit my daughter and bring her clothes and presents for Christmas.

As soon as I got home, my stepbrother handed me a pistol because E. St. Louis, by this time, was infested with crackheads, and it had gotten so bad that people did not even stop at stop signs, and the traffic lights were flashing yellow at night as the crime rate was at its peak and people were afraid of stopping even at the stop signals because of it.

Seeing what happened to my home, I felt bad from the depths of my heart. I visited Blue at his parents' house and met Buddy as he had returned to E. St. Louis.

After that, I went to the rice house on State Street to get some fried rice. I was about to pay for the rice at the window when a crackhead came behind me with a pistol in his hand and tried to jack me up for my money. When Buddy saw the incident, he jumped in and grabbed his pistol and shouted, "Not today, partner, not today!" while pointing his pistol at him. The crackhead got scared and ran away. I thought I was going to be killed that day, but Buddy saved my life.

The next day, I was with my stepbrother driving to Milwaukee, Wisconsin, but on the way, we stopped in Chicago to meet with our cousins Greg and Steve Franklin. Greg and Steve decided to ride with us to Milwaukee as we were going to meet my daughter. When we got to my daughter's grandmother's house, I went up and knocked on the door. However, it came as a surprise when the grandmother came to the door but refused to open the door and asked me to go away. She told me that she would not allow me to see my daughter.

After hearing that, I got infuriated as she could have told me that before I drove all the way from E. St. Louis to Milwaukee. How could she not let me meet my daughter? I wanted to meet her and give her Christmas presents and the clothes that I had bought for her. However, my stepbrother and cousins calmed me down. Feeling helpless, I just took all the boxes, set them outside the main door, and left.

We dropped our cousins in Chicago and went back to E. St. Louis. Once again, I was ready to get the hell out of E. St. Louis and was happy that my plane was leaving the next day.

While in E. St. Louis, I ran into my childhood friend who went to Assumption High School. She had moved to Atlanta and came back to visit her family in E. St. Louis. She had to attend her sorority homecoming and invited me to join her. So, I went to her sorority party and had a good time there. At the party, I also bumped into some of my former classmates from E. St. Louis Senior High School.

I spent the whole night there enjoying myself with my friends and came back home the next day at 8 in the morning as my flight was scheduled for 10:30 am, and I also had to return the rental car.

When I walked in, my parents were having their morning coffee, and I did not really get a chance to spend time with them before I left that morning. I remember my mother asking me if I enjoyed my visit and my father saying, "It looked like he enjoyed himself last night." I was a little embarrassed, but I had to leave as I had a flight to catch.

I was about to start a new year; it was the beginning of 1990. I was back in San Diego and went back to my routine at the NCO School. When I came back, I came to know that my girlfriend's brother was visiting her from out of town. He was riding a bike when he was hit by a car, which took his life.

My girlfriend was devastated and needed my love, support, and care, but unfortunately, I had to return to work at the NCO School.

In the little time I had, I tried to console her, but it was not enough, and I knew it because she was hurting. I believe that put a strain on our relationship, but we were still together.

Finally, my promotion to SSgt. got approved, and I became an SSgt. on April 4, 1990. At the same time, I re-enlisted for six years.

I checked out of NCO School on April 8, 1990, and prepared to leave for Okinawa on April 14, 1990. I sold my car to a marine and moved out of my apartment. My girlfriend gave me a lift to LAX so I could head back to Okinawa. We got there a day early to spend some quality time together before we said goodbye to each other. Neither of us wanted to be separated, and we were determined to keep the long-distance relationship until I was back in the States. But time flew quickly, and the next day arrived – I was on the plane to Okinawa.

Chapter 16: Okinawa, Desert Storm, and Back to Drill Instructor Duty

On April 15, 1990, I landed back in Okinawa, Japan, and was assigned to the 3rd Marine Division, 12th Marines Artillery Battery. When I checked in to 12th Marines, the Sgt.Maj. assigned me to be the Enlisted Barracks Staff-NCO.

I didn't want to be the Barracks Staff NCO because, in my opinion, it was a worthless job with nothing much to do. However, the Sgt.Maj. insisted that since I had just come from being an instructor at the NCO School, I deserved a break.

So, I became the Barracks Staff-NCO, where I had to actually manage the barracks where the enlisted marines lived with the ranks from private to sergeant. Upon inspecting the operation of the Barracks, I discovered that two Corporals named Cpl. Hyde and Cpl. Clark were already running the Barracks and were doing an outstanding job. Therefore, I just let them do their jobs and did not interrupt.

I went back to the Sgt.Maj. and told him about the two Corporals, but he was not convinced and told me to stay as the Barracks Staff NCO, so I did.

So, here I was, living in the staff NCO quarters on the other side of the base at Camp Foster. It was the third time I was stationed in Okinawa on Camp Foster.

One day, on my way back from the Chow Hall, I looked across the street and saw Anthony Moore heading to the Chow Hall. Yes, the same Cpl. Moore from South Philly who used to be the driver for the Commanding General 1st MAW, but now he was a Sgt. When he first saw me, he nearly passed out in disbelief.

We were both very surprised as well as pleased to see each other. We exchanged our contact information so we could hang out later. That same day, I also ran into my ex-wife, who also happened to be stationed in Okinawa. We met and talked about our little girl. I was surprised when she informed me that she was engaged and was soon going to marry. I thought, '*Wow, that was quick, but whatever,*' and moved past it.

I spent some time with Sgt. Tony Moore in nightclubs and jazz clubs in the town. I found out that he was just coming off Embassy Duty and was stationed in Egypt and Kenya. Also, he had recently gotten married, and his Kenyan wife was living in the States with his relatives.

After about a couple of weeks in Okinawa, I received a letter from my girlfriend back in the States stating that she wanted to talk to me on the phone. Fortunately, Tony had a phone in his room and I asked him if I could use his phone.

After so many years, I still don't know how Tony wired a phone to connect to his room, as no one I knew at the camp had a landline phone in their room, but he did. Anyhow, a few days later, I gave my girlfriend a call using the phone in Tony's room.

As soon as I called her, she started crying, and when I asked her the reason, she said, "He said he loves me." After hearing that, I was shocked. Imagine your girlfriend telling you someone was telling her they loved her.

"What did you say?" I asked her. Still crying, she said again, "He said he loves me."

Still reeling from the shock, I asked if she loved him back, and she replied, "Yes." I was curious. I wanted to know who this man was who had swept my girlfriend off her feet while I wasn't around. I asked her about him, and she told me he was a co-worker.

Suddenly, something clicked in my mind, and I asked her if he was the guy who only dated white girls, and she replied in the affirmative.

I was totally shocked and somewhat brokenhearted, but there wasn't much I could do – she was in love with someone else, someone who seemingly loved her back equally, if not more. I didn't want her to be alone, so I told her, "Do what is best for you." She was still crying and apologizing, so I told her, "Look, you have to look out for yourself, so again, do what is best for you."

Then, I told her that I had to go and hung up the phone. Tony asked me if everything was fine, and I responded, "Man, you won't believe what just happened to me. I just received a 'Dear John' phone call, can you believe that? She told me she was in love with another man, and that man confessed his love for her, so I told her to do what was best for her and hung up the phone."

"Damn," was the only word that came out of Tony's mouth, and then he asked me if I wanted a drink. It was only 8:30 in the morning, so that was how we spent the rest of our time in Okinawa, drinking our days away.

***

Since I had nothing much to do on the camp as the two corporals ran the barracks, I moved off base into an apartment. I started dating multiple women as I had lost the respect I once had for them after what happened to me again.

I dated women in the Air Force, Army, Marines, and the local Okinawa women as well. Hell, I was even dating married women. I was doing all this because I thought it would make me feel better, but my heart still remained broken.

I spent a lot of time with Tony, mostly at the NCO club on Kadina Air Base and at Japanese clubs in the city of Naha. We often hung out at a club named "TEMPS." The owner loved Motown music and named his club after the Temptations. His other private club, which was only for the Okinawans, was called "Motown."

Fortunately, the owner liked me and allowed me in both of his clubs anytime I wanted, that, too, with no cover charge. The owner would always have a table set for me and my crew. Tony and I used to stay until the club closed, which was around 2 am, and then we would head over to the afterparty in Motown until 6 in the morning.

We were able to do that since neither of us had a job that required us to be present there regularly.

I moved into a different apartment, but this time, with a roommate, and that place became our party spot. I remember the day when they closed TEMPS at 6 in the morning, and I was driving with Tony and the other guys when I asked, "Who wants to ride shotgun?"

One of the guys said that he wanted to volunteer, and as we were in Tony's car heading back north close to the base, all of them were half asleep, including Tony, who was in the driving seat. But by the grace of God, the bumps on the side of the highway on the cliff woke Tony just in time, and he steered us back onto the road before we could head off of the cliff.

Tony slammed on the brakes and got out of the car, cursing the guy who wanted to ride shotgun. Tony kept yelling at him because he went to sleep because if you rode shotgun, your main responsibility was keeping the driver awake.

Although we had almost died, I could not stop laughing because Tony, though he was the driver, blamed everything on the other guy in our crew and cursed him out the entire way home.

When we returned to the apartment, all of us took a power nap for about three to four hours. We started our next day with a barbeque, drinking, and clubbing. This became our routine for the next nine months while I continued dating multiple women, trying to forget about the "Dear John" phone call from my ex.

Finally, in December 1990, I received orders to report back to the Marine Corps Recruit Depot (MCRD), San Diego, CA, for another tour of Drill Instructor duty. I was shocked after seeing that my reporting date was February, which only gave me ten months in Okinawa, but I was happy that I was going back to the drill field.

In December of the same year, I was almost arrested by the Military Police for fleeing the scene of an accident. What happened was that I was attending a Christmas party with Double-A at a marine's house, and we got intoxicated and decided to take a taxi on our way back. I went back to my apartment, and Double-A went back to his barracks. I left my car at the house along with my keys just in case they needed to move it.

However, I received a call from the homeowners that my car was missing along with my key; someone had taken my car. My blood was boiling in anger; how could someone just take my car. So, I called the Military Police to report that my car had been stolen.

The next thing I knew, the Military Police was knocking at my door at 4 in the morning. They asked me to put my clothes on and come to the station. Apparently, whoever was driving my car was involved in an accident and had fled the scene.

Of course, they thought it was me and Double-A because two people were seen in the car during the accident. I asked them to call Double-A so he could vouch for me and himself as well, but they did not believe us.

They brought Double-A to the station and questioned us for hours in separate rooms. I was told that whoever was in my car was in traffic, and when they tried to back up, they inadvertently hit the bus that was behind them and then left the scene.

I asked them where my car was and if there was any damage, to which they replied that they had not located the car and I hid it somewhere and got a taxi home.

Once again, I was in a police station in Okinawa. It seemed like history really enjoyed repeating itself with me. They finally let us go but informed us that they would continue the investigation. As I was leaving, I told them I just wanted my car back, and they should be able to find it because we were on an Island.

As unbelievable as it may sound, they never found my car, so I had to use one of my roommates' cars until it was time for me to move to my next duty station.

During my last two months in Okinawa, Desert Storm kicked off, and I was finally given a real job in my MOS as a warehouse chief.

The 12th Marine Artillery unit was ordered to report to Saudi Arabia within a month. As a warehouse chief, my duty was to make sure we had all the necessary supplies ready to go when it was time to ship off.

I was working really hard with my team to get everything perfect and ready to go. The SgtMaj. called me into his office to discuss my orders. He told me I would not be joining the unit in Saudi Arabia, which upset me. I told him that I wanted to stay with the unit and go to Saudi Arabia. He explained to me that there were only two orders that could not be canceled during wartime, and those orders were for recruiters and drill instructors.

Therefore, I got my unit ready to go and watched them get shipped off to Saudi Arabia while I headed back to San Diego. As upset as I was for not being able to go to Saudi Arabia with my unit, it was also a blessing in disguise because I later found out that most of the marines in my unit who returned home from Saudi Arabia had severe respiratory issues because of what they were breathing in after firing artillery shells. Some of them told me that whatever was in those shells was blowing right back into their face because of the direction of the wind.

So, I learned that we must be careful of what we ask for and realized that God was looking out for me.

When I was checking out with the Military Police, I enquired about my vehicle, but to no avail. They never found my car nor charged me with leaving the scene of the accident.

During this time, I was dating an Okinawan woman who was a model, a beautiful one, to be specific. She wanted to come back to the United States with me, but I could not even imagine bringing her back to the US to deal with all of the challenges that we would be faced with, so I said goodbye to her and flew back to San Diego alone.

February 21, 1991, was the day I reported back to the MCRD Drill Instructor School. Surprisingly, the Drill Master at the DI School was my old chief instructor at NCO School, GySgt. Colon.

The SgtMaj. of DI School knew my history and tried to deny me from challenging the Board. By challenging the board, all prior drill instructors could choose not to go through the whole DI School training or could complete drill instructor school in thirty days.

Thankfully, GySgt. Colon called them out and told them how unfair it would be to deny me from challenging the Board, so they allowed me to do it, which I did; I graduated from Drill Instructor School in thirty days.

It was tough because I was out of shape as I had spent ten months drinking and clubbing in Okinawa instead of working out, but I made it and graduated from DI School in March 1990.

That was the moment I knew what I wanted to accomplish as a drill instructor with GySgt. Colon. I loved working with GySgt. Colon and being an instructor at DI school — it was a dream come true.

After graduating, I was assigned to the 2nd Battalion, Echo Company, the same company I graduated from while in Boot Camp. Since I was a former Drill Instructor, they expected a lot from me. So, I hit the ground running so that I could fulfill the expectations they had of me.

After a while, I contacted my ex-girlfriend to see if there was any chance that we could get back together, but that was not going to happen because she was now engaged to be married.

At first, I was disappointed, but when I thought about it, she was better off with him because I would never have married her anyway. I had to be honest with myself and understand the only reason I was hurting was that I was not the one who ended the relationship; she was!

Chapter 17: Second Tour as a Drill Instructor, Getting Burnt Out, Honorable Discharge, and Reentering Civilian Life

A sports car with only two seats had been on my bucket list for a long time. So, when I returned to San Diego, the first thing I did was buy a Mazda RX7. A new start in San Diego called for a new vehicle, after all. I modified the car three times to get the right midnight blue with sparkles that were only visible during the day. I also got specialized license plates that stated my intentions for the rest of my life: "SOLOIST." I was surprised that they were available at DMV. Everyone around me was familiar with my car. When I checked into Echo Company, I heard other Drill instructors wondering who that car belonged to.

As I began a new chapter of my life, I realized I was a different person now than on my first tour. The DI cover and the rank did not mean much to me this time. It was all about who I was as a person and a leader. Therefore, I never looked at an officer or an enlisted person's rank; it was all about their character.

People thought I was overconfident, but I was very grateful for the opportunity to become a Drill Instructor again. I took this chance seriously and grew a lot along the process. I didn't become proud or arrogant because of my position as a DI. I was teaching new trainees how to improve, and now I had to teach other Drill Instructors too. However, after being away for a couple of years, I found that DIs weren't as strong as they used to be. They were more like glorified babysitters, and I couldn't accept that. So, I pushed the new training recruits and the DIs to do their best. I treated other DIs respectfully - I was never disrespectful; I just helped them be true to themselves while being DIs.

When I started working at the Company, they put me on teams that could have been better. I mostly just watched from the sidelines and was surprised by how nice the DIs were to new recruits. I had to double-check myself because some Drill Instructors thought I was crazy when I pushed new recruits hard. But this was the way we did it three years ago.

However, I had to agree with what everyone else was doing and conform to the status quo. After some time, I joined my third platoon. There, I was assigned to a different team consisting only of Senior DI SSgt James, DI SSgt Medina, and myself, DI SSgt Cason. The Senior DI, SSgt James, allowed me and SSgt Medina to take over the Platoon and train them in the way we thought was best, and we trained them a lot. I enjoyed training recruits the way I was trained when I started my military service. I liked this team because we all supported each other, and we knew it. While in the other teams, everyone feared someone might make a mistake and get in trouble. A DI team can only do well if everyone trusts each other, and that's what we did.

Everyone who finished training with this group became a United States Marine. We did well when the Company evaluated our Platoon's performance in Drill, Physical Fitness, and Practical Examination. We were always the best platoon in the Company. We did everything we could to train recruits and succeed, as long as it followed the rules and guidelines. When the DIs broke the rules, they were removed from their job and punished in court like I did when I got busted on my first tour. But in my case, the Battalion Commander was out to get me. However, this team did extremely well, breaking previous records and becoming the Honor Platoon.

As a single Drill Instructor, I lived in a one-bedroom apartment on base. People knew me as a strict but fun DI who worked and enjoyed life equally. Work hard and play hard was my motto, and when I had time off, I played very hard.

As the SOLOIST, I promised never to be in a serious relationship again, and I kept that promise. People thought of me as someone who always had women coming in and going out of his room. But in my defense, I was always upfront with them about my intentions. I never lied and always told the truth to everyone I dated.

One night, I spent time with an old friend named Tony Reaves, who also taught at the NCO School. While we were at a bar, Tupac Shakur sat beside me. Tupac Shakur was traveling with Digital Underground back then and had just released his first music album called 2Pacalypse Now. I enjoyed his music, and we chatted for about 15 minutes. Tupac asked me why I joined the Marine Corps, and I told him it was because I was from E. St. Louis.

"I understand," he said.

Curious about his statement, I asked him if he knew about E. St. Louis, and he replied, "Yes."

Anyway, we continued talking, and I told Tupac I liked his album and encouraged him to continue making good music. Tony saw me talking to someone, and when he got closer, he realized who it was.

"Tupac!" he shouted, coming toward us.

"Tupac, my man, what's going on?" he said excitedly.

Tupac said it was nice conversing with me. We greeted each other, and he went back to perform on the stage. So that was how I met Tupac, one of the best poetic rappers of all time. I completed two more platoons with SSgt James and SSgt Medina before SSgt Medina went to Camp Pendleton. Normally, someone with prior experience as a DI would have been a senior after one platoon, but it seems people had heard about my reputation from my first tour. I didn't care about being a junior DI because you got to do most of the training. After SSgt Medina left, I picked up two more platoons with SSgt James in charge, and we kept doing great. Things were going well until, all of a sudden, the leadership changed, and all hell broke loose.

One day, I was asked to go to the Company Office about a check I got for traveling after returning from Okinawa. Since my ex-wife and I were both in Okinawa at the same time, they thought our daughter was there too and added dependent pay to my check. Truth be told, I hadn't even opened the check until weeks later, and even then, I didn't pay much attention to it and deposited it. That was a mistake I made, and now I had to pay the price for it because the Company Commanding Officer accused me of lying and demanded that I have office hours.

Of course, that wasn't true, but the 1stSgt recommended that I just take the office hours and go back to work.

I remember having flashbacks from my first tour. Not ready to have a repeat of that situation, I asked the 1stSgt if he was joking and questioned the accounting clerk's competence. He agreed it was unjust but could not do anything about it.

I said that I believed the 1stSgt was supposed to support his enlisted personnel. The 1stSgt, who happened to be a redneck, lost his cool at that and said I should be court-martialed. I knew the so-called leadership didn't have my back, so I accepted the Commanding Officer's NJP: a fine and confinement to the barracks for two weeks, which he later decided not to enforce.

Without a good leader, everyone in an organization gets affected. SSgt James was promoted to Chief Drill Instructor, and I had to go to a different platoon as a junior DI. So, I decided to take things my way and did what I used to do. I taught new recruits the same way I did with SSgt James, but the new Senior DI wanted more control and thought I was trying to take charge of the platoon. Even though the Company's working conditions got worse, I still kept working hard and giving my best.

It was almost as if the Senior DI was competing with me about who was the more popular DI on the team. He didn't like me and made up false stories about me to make himself look good, but I ignored him and focused on doing my job.

One day in Phase 3, I was requalifying on the rifle range at Camp Pendleton. The last day after I qualified, a horrible accident took place on Interstate 5 between Camp Pendleton and MCRD San Diego. It took me almost four hours to return to MCRD from Camp Pendleton. When I returned to MCRD, I went to my room to change because I had duty that night. The new Senior DI came to my room very angry and asked me why I wasn't at the place where I had been and why I wasn't at the Duty Hut. I told him about the accident, but he didn't believe me and started to accuse me of drinking and not doing my job.

I couldn't believe he was accusing me of such a thing, so I told him to check the news or go to the hospital to prove I wasn't drinking. At that moment, I lost the little bit of respect I had for him, even though we were supposed to be like brothers. To be honest, that is what our Company had become. People felt like the only way they could get ahead was to report someone for something.

I had to constantly look over my shoulder for the rest of the cycle, and it made me uncomfortable. But I had to do it for the recruits I taught. I clarified to the Company that I wanted to work with someone other than that Senior DI. At that point, I had already done seven platoons, which was unheard of for a former DI. Still, I chose to come back but wasn't given a chance to be an instructor at DI School, so I just did my normal job. When the people in charge left, I wanted to avoid being involved with the Echo Company. I also felt tired and burned out.

Guess what? President Clinton approved a program to make the US Military smaller. So, if you had a certain job and rank in the military, you could request an early discharge and also be entitled to severance pay if your request was approved. My MOS and rank allowed me to ask for an early discharge, which is what I did.

My request was approved within a few months. I was now a Senior DI and ready to lead another platoon. I informed Echo Company I was about to be discharged from the Marine Corps and even showed them the paperwork, but they didn't believe me. At the briefing, they still had me assigned as a Senior DI, and I reminded them that I would be leaving the military soon, but they didn't do anything about it. As I mentioned, no one was in charge of the Echo Company at that point. So, they asked me to lead another group of recruits, even though I would be leaving the Marine Corps in a month.

The minute I found out my discharge request had been approved, I started searching for an apartment and a job in San Diego because I wanted to return there. I asked my old Marine Corps friend, Ron Barr, who had a career in San Diego, for advice on finding work. He told me about Continental Graphics, where he worked as a data analyst, and suggested I apply there. I asked him what a data analyst does. He answered that Continental Graphics created an Illustrated Parts Catalogue (IPC) for Boeing and McDonnell Douglas airplanes.

I was told that data analysts examine airplane designs and identify individual parts, which they then record on a computer. The illustrator then draws them and puts them into the IPC. I told him I had never done that kind of job before, but he said they would send me to school if I was hired, so I applied for the job. I was interviewed and hired while still in the Marine Corps.

My final month in the marines was very hectic. I had to go through the discharge process while simultaneously taking charge of a new platoon as a Senior DI and searching for a new place to stay and work. I didn't let the fact that there was no leadership at Echo Company stop me from leaving. After my team picked up a new platoon, I talked to my junior DIs about what was happening. I told them what they needed to do to ensure the new recruits did well because I would not be around any longer. The Company didn't trust or believe that my opinion was necessary.

One afternoon, I was leaving and finishing up the paperwork. Suddenly, the Echo Company realized that I was telling the truth, and I was about to get honorably discharged. They asked the Chief DI and the Series Commander why I had been allowed to pick up another platoon. They came up with many reasons, but the Chief DI was upset. So, he told the Company Commander he didn't know about my discharge papers and tried to charge me with unauthorized absence (UA). But of course, they knew he was lying since the paperwork didn't lie. His plans failed, and he was reprimanded for his lack of knowledge of his DIs.

With only two weeks to go, they needed to find another Senior DI to take charge of the platoon, and I had to explain why to the platoon because I felt like they deserved clarity.

On my last day as their Senior DI, I told them they'd get another Senior DI, and I promised to attend their graduation.

For the next two weeks, I did important things like attending classes for my new job, looking for a home, and buying things to put inside it. Thankfully, my friend Julian Alston had also been honorably discharged from the military and now lived in San Diego while working with a furniture company. So, I got a lower price on my furniture because of him.

I needed to pack my things, but after my time in the Marine Corps, I didn't want to take anything with me that would remind me of it. So, I got rid of all my uniforms and things that reminded me of my time in the Marine Corps. I gave all my old furniture and vinyl records to others. I only kept one of my DI Covers and nothing else.

I managed to find a small one-bedroom in Downtown San Diego on B St. This was a relatively new apartment with a fireplace and a great kitchen. I remember signing a one-year lease for $475 monthly.

Finally, the day that I was waiting for arrived. I left the United States Marine Corps on October 1, 1992, after serving for 12 years and four months. I remember that day well; it feels like it happened only yesterday. When I first came in, I was 17 years old. Now, I was 29 years old, starting afresh.

I was thrilled about it. I promised myself I wouldn't think about things that happened to me before, and I kept my promise. I left the military and received my severance pay. I drove off base for the last time, and it felt great. I was now a civilian!

Transitioning into non-military life was easy for me because I had stopped caring about people's rank a long time ago and focused on who they were. I went to live in the condo I had leased and completed the training Continental Graphics gave me before I began my new job as a data analyst.

I had fun working at Continental Graphics. It was a big company with many workers, so I met many new people and made some new friends, too. Something that surprised me was my boss, Mark Grey. Mark was a young manager at the company who was getting promoted fast. He was very impressive because he always remained calm in any situation. I was not used to living like a regular person, and my bosses in the Marine Corps would often yell at me for something. However, Mark's way of leading made me pause and consider it more carefully. I thought Mark was great, and everyone else thought so, too. Going to work was enjoyable, which had not been the case in a while.

I was still single and lived alone in downtown San Diego. My friends and I used to think that my life was perfect. I went out with pretty girls, but we weren't serious, and I was still free to do what I wanted. Eventually, I began a romantic relationship with a person from work whom I met during our training. She was a pretty lady from the Philippines who had been transferred from another location of Continental Graphics. We began going out and spending more time together, but she preferred to keep it a secret. I was okay with that because I had two other secret relationships at the time.

Continental Graphics was a huge company; we had different sports teams like basketball, softball, bowling, and flag football. So, I played a lot in different teams, especially bowling and basketball. I played in a basketball league in the spring and summer. I was happy because I won two games in a row by making the last shot before the game ended. I also scored the most points in a game that season. In one game, I scored 32 points. Pretty good for a brother who couldn't make the team in high school. Things were going well, and life felt good.

Echo Company Drill Instructor

2nd Tour as a Marine Drill Instructor

Chapter 18: From Emptiness to God Answering My Prayers

Life was going well for me; I had quickly settled into my civilian life and was enjoying it. Work at Continental Graphics was also going great, and so was my relationship with my Filipino girlfriend. But of course, judging by my past experiences, I should have known that when things seemed too good to be true, there was surely a storm brewing in the background.

One day, out of the blue, my girlfriend mentioned that she wanted to go public with our relationship, even though we had been okay with keeping it private. When I asked her why she wanted to do that all of a sudden, she said she didn't really care who knew about our relationship.

At that point in time, I didn't mind it either, and so we went public. We would go out for lunch, go out for walks during breaks, and even come to work together in the mornings. Within a few weeks, everyone at work knew we were an item. I should mention here that some of her Filipino friends weren't really happy with our relationship, but I didn't find it odd. I just figured it was because of jealousy or feeling protective of their friend.

Later on, I found out that my girlfriend had been trying to prove a point by going public, and I was just a pawn in that game. Anyway, the days went by, and a few months after we went public, my girlfriend came over to my apartment one day and informed me that she was pregnant. To say I was shocked was an understatement. I had still not recovered from the scars of my previous relationships, and now she had presented me with this startling news.

Before I even had time to process the news, she went ahead and informed me that she would be getting an abortion. That came as an even bigger shock: that she would take that decision on her own without even consulting with me or asking me how I felt about it. I asked her to wait and talk things through, but she was adamant about going ahead with it. When I realized that there was no talking her out of it, I asked her why she was so hellbent on getting an abortion – that was when the cat came out of the bag.

My girlfriend revealed that she was married. She had initially married to obtain a visa, but when her husband turned out to be abusive, she requested a transfer to San Diego. She went on to tell me that this was not the first time she had become pregnant, and if she had this child, it would ruin her chances of ever obtaining her visa.

I was blown away and in shock at the same time – it was too much to take in. I didn't know how to respond, but I didn't want her to have an abortion either, so pushing my emotions aside, I tried to talk some sense into her. I assured her that we would figure things out together and that I was in this for the long haul. However, she wasn't willing to listen. I guess that didn't go over so well with her because, after that, she told me we needed to stop seeing each other as I was jeopardizing her visa.

I was astounded by her nonchalant behavior. All she was concerned about was her visa. What about our time together? What about the life she was carrying inside her? Did it mean nothing to her? Was it so easy for her to push it all aside just to get citizenship?

I was at a loss for words, and she had already decided what she was going to do, so I don't think there was anything I could have said that would have made a difference. She gathered her things and left; that was that.

The next few weeks were horrible. I felt betrayed and used, and my heart was completely shattered. Not only that, but I had to continue to work with my now ex-girlfriend and see her on a daily basis. I can't explain what it felt like seeing her every day, knowing she was carrying our child.

I tried to reach out to her multiple times, but to no avail, as she always ignored my phone calls. She wouldn't even acknowledge me at work, which hurt me to the core. I had never experienced this kind of heartbreak before.

One day, she informed me of when she was scheduled for an abortion. Once again, I tried to talk her out of it, but there was no convincing her. On that fateful day, she was absent from work, and it felt awful knowing where she was. Just the thought of what was happening made me sick, so I left work early and headed to a bar in downtown San Diego, downing drink after drink. I cried; I was hurting not just for me but for my unborn child and what could have been. To make matters worse, I realized my own actions had led me down this road. I was using her just as much as she was using me.

What the hell was I doing? I asked myself again and again, but I couldn't come up with a satisfactory response.

I saw her again the next Monday, and while I had lost all respect for her, I can't lie and say it didn't hurt. After that, I stopped dating altogether. I stopped seeing the women I used to from time to time and just wanted to be left alone.

I realized I had to do some soul-searching, and that led me to accept responsibility for my selfish actions, understanding that whatever I did had consequences. I knew I had hurt people in the past, but I had no idea that it hurt this much. You know what they say; what goes around comes around, and karma really is a bitch.

As time went by, I started getting used to being alone and was not looking to start dating anytime soon. Days turned into months, and I started looking at women differently. I did not intend to ever use them like the old Ced would have. It wasn't like I didn't have ample opportunities, being a bachelor living in a condo in downtown San Diego. But whenever the opportunity arose, my conscience told me I wasn't ready yet and warned me from returning to being that person who had never been heartbroken.

I didn't want to put anybody through what I had gone through, so I kept my distance. In fact, one evening, I went into my closet, got on my knees, and prayed to God. I asked God for forgiveness and that if there was anyone out there for me, please send her to me. I was alone, and I didn't want to be alone anymore, but I was also done with the physical relationships. I wanted something solid, something permanent.

So, I left the matter to God and continued to go about my life. I went to work, played on all the sports leagues at work, and just hung out with the fellas.

As months passed, I got a call one day from Anthony Moore (Tony), my old Marine Corps buddy from Okinawa. This was back in May 1994. Tony was back in the US and was stationed at Camp Pendleton, CA, with his wife, whom he met while on embassy duty in Kenya. Tony invited me to a barbeque he was having at his base-housing unit on Camp Pendleton. I immediately turned him down, saying it had only been a couple of years and I had no plans to go to a Marine Corps base anytime soon. He told me that he had been in touch with Allen Hyde (Double A), the other brother we hung out with in Okinawa, who was also stationed locally, and he wanted us both to come to his house for a reunion.

I wasn't ready to reconnect with people in the Marine Corps because I had left that life and hurt behind me – or so I thought. Tony kept calling me, and he even had Double A call me to convince me to show up, saying he would only go if I went. I eventually gave in because I had nothing planned for the day of the reunion. That Saturday, I picked up Double-A and drove to Camp Pendleton for the Okinawa reunion.

I don't remember the exact reason for the barbeque, but Tony and his wife Njeri had invited other people, so it was a houseful of people. Njeri introduced me to her girlfriend from Kenya, whom she worked with as a flight attendant at Pan Am. Her name was Rachel, and she was living in San Diego at the time.

Rachel was attractive, but I wasn't attracted to her because I wasn't looking for anyone and was not ready to go down that road again anytime soon. Since Double-A and I had brought a fifth of scotch, and Tony had already had a fifth of scotch, we got pretty drunk that evening, so we decided that we would have to spend the night at Tony's base housing on Camp Pendelton.

I awoke the next morning to the smell of breakfast cooking and a slight headache. Njeri and Rachel were preparing breakfast; it smelt very good and tasted even better. Double-A and I ate and then left, heading back to San Diego. The next weekend, Tony came down to San Diego to pay me a visit, and we hung out for half the day.

***

There came a time when I felt traveling for work was a hassle, so I decided to move closer to work. I started looking for places and eventually found an apartment in Mira Mesa, CA. My roommate, Patrick Sieyes, happened to be a coworker at Continental Graphics. He had been discharged from the Navy, and we became good friends from being roommates. We were both single; therefore, we gave each other space, and the arrangement worked out well for us.

The next month, it was Njeri's birthday weekend, and they were having another barbeque. I was invited again, but this time, I went willingly. I had a good time socializing and eating and noticed that Rachel was giving me a lot of attention. However, even though it had been more than six months since I had last seen anyone, I still wasn't ready to start dating again, so I didn't take the bait.

As per tradition, Tony and I got really drunk and stayed up listening to Jazz. I ended up spending the night at their place again. The next morning, after breakfast, I was getting ready to leave when Njeri asked me if I could give Rachel a ride home since she lived in San Diego. I agreed.

I dropped Rachel off at her apartment in North Park, San Diego, and the ride was uneventful. She was working at Bullocks in Mission Valley, and we exchanged numbers just in case I was heading back up to see Tony and Njeri, and she needed a ride.

Some time went by, and she called me one day. After that, we started talking on the phone regularly. The next thing I knew, we were planning to have dinner together, and I decided to take her to Sizzler. I ordered a drink, and Rachel ordered a Long Island iced tea. They brought biscuits and we sipped on our drinks, talked, and nibbled on the biscuits. It didn't take too long for Rachel to get tipsy, and when I say she was tipsy, I mean she was DRUNK. She had only drunk about a fourth of her Long Island iced tea before she could hardly sit up straight. I asked her if she had ever had a Long Island iced tea before, and she shook her head. Needless to say, we had to skip dinner. I took Rachel back to her apartment, tucked her in, locked her door, and went back to my place.

The next day, I called to check up on her. She was embarrassed, but I didn't mind. I could tell she didn't know what she was ordering the other night. Anyway, we talked on the phone regularly, and it got to the point where we were calling each other every single day. We went out to see a movie and had dinner a few times, but I was still not ready to get into a relationship. However, it was nice to hang out with Rachel because she was really fun. I even invited her to a company gathering which she attended and had a good time.

We were becoming close friends, and I was cool with that. Not soon after Njeri's birthday, Tony and Njeri were having another "hang," as Kenyans called them, and, of course, Tony invited me again. I said yes, and deep down, I was hoping Rachel would also come. Much to my delight, she did.

Things at the gathering went down as usual; Tony and I stayed up late drinking and listening to Jazz. The next morning, it was obvious Rachel was giving me a lot of attention, and I could see that it was bothering Njeri as she was very protective of Rachel. Njeri didn't want Rachel to get a ride home with me again, and she let it be known.

Now, the thing was, I had a two-seater, and Double-A happened to be with me this time around, so I could only give one person a ride to San Diego. We had to use multiple cars, and when it was time to go, Rachel decided to go with me. Njeri was surprised and wanted to know what was going on between us. I just shrugged and pointed to Rachel, indicating that she should ask her.

Anyway, Rachel rode back with me. I wanted to show her my new apartment, but Njeri didn't miss the chance and told me they would be right behind us because they all wanted to see my new apartment. So, the whole gang came over to my new apartment, and I introduced them to my new roommate, Patrick.

While we were all sitting and chatting, I told Rachel about the company picnic we were going to have that afternoon and asked her if she would go with me. She said yes.

We took a blanket and a cooler and went to Admiral Bakers Park to attend the company picnic. Laying down, I fell asleep at some point, and when I came to, Rachel was staring at me from above, to my surprise. That was the first time I thought we might have something going on, but I was still hesitant. I believe it was that evening when I took Rachel home that we shared our first kiss. We started hanging out more after that.

One day, I was picking up Rachel from work; I couldn't see her until I got closer and saw her for the first time without her weaved-in hair extensions. "Well, hello, my name is Cedric, and what's your name?" I walked up to her and said. We shared a good laugh over that. She looked totally different, but she was still beautiful.

Soon, she introduced me to her friends in San Diego, Wanjiru, and Murugi, who were both from Kenya and were roommates attending the International University in San Diego. We all hit it off very well and enjoyed the Jazz scene. I was known to hang out at the Jazz Happy Hours all around San Diego. Some of my favorites to follow were Hollis

Gentry and Fattburger. Some of my favorite spots were Humphrey's by the Bay, Red Onion, Hilton on the Bay, and the Rusty Pelican. I loved the Jazz scene in San Diego because just about everyone knew each other or recognized each other.

One Saturday, we were to meet Wanjiru and Murugi at the Rusty Pelican for brunch, and that is when I met Kamau Kenyatta for the first time. I had seen and heard him play before but never met him. He knew Wanjiru and Murugi. I knew Hollis because I used to follow his band around the Jazz scene because that brother could play the Sax like I never heard before, and he reminded me of Miles Davis. It was sad when I heard that he had passed away.

***

Once again, we were hanging out at Tony and Njeri's house on Camp Pendleton. Rachel and I were having a discussion about each other's future, and I had no idea where mine was headed at that time. However, Rachel had other ideas, and they involved being married. I had no idea what came over me, but I asked Rachel if she wouldn't mind coming upstairs with me, and she agreed.

Once we got upstairs, I told her that if we were going to do this, I needed to know if she was willing to get on her knees and pray with me then and there. Her eyes started watering, and she said yes. So, we both got on our knees, and I prayed to God, asking for His guidance in our decision and for His blessings, His protection, and His Wisdom for making decisions together and moving forward in JESUS's name.

We were both crying as we did and when we got up and hugged each other, I said, "Yes, I will marry you." That was when I realized that God had answered the prayer that I had prayed in my closet over a year ago. To GOD be the Glory!

"When I was a child, I used to talk as a child, think as a child, reason as a child; when I became a man, I put aside childish things." 1 Corinthians 13:11

Chapter 19: Time for Change
(Marriage, New Job, New Beginnings, Moving up the Ladder)

As the year was winding down, excitement and anticipation filled my heart. It was Thanksgiving 1994 when Rachel and I decided to take our relationship to the next level and get engaged. It was a moment of joy and love that we chose to cherish privately for the time being. Life in San Diego was going well, or so I thought. I had worked hard, but disappointment washed over me like a tidal wave when the much-awaited raises came through. After two years of dedication and working as a Senior Engineering Data Analyst for $7 an hour, a mere ten-cent increase felt like treachery. The frustration was overwhelming, and I knew it was time for me to switch. With a heavy heart but a determined spirit, I walked up to my boss, Mark, and handed him my resignation letter. It was liberating to remember that, unlike my time in the Marine Corps, I was not bound by any contract. I was free to choose my future, and I decided to leave. As I stood there on my last day at Continental Graphics, emotions swirled within me like a storm. Two years of hard work, dedication, and loyalty were met with a measly ten-cent raise. But I also felt something else brewing inside me—a sense of liberation and the hope that better days would come.

I reached out to an old roommate, Julian, who had found a job at a furniture company in Anaheim, CA. He mentioned another opportunity in Irvine, CA, and I tried it. The only hurdle was finding a place to stay until I settled in. Julian kindly offered me his hospitality, and I gladly accepted.

When I shared the news with Rachel that I was moving to Orange County, her response was unexpected yet heartwarming. Without hesitating, she declared, "Then I'm going too." Her unwavering support and commitment touched my soul, and I knew she was someone I could count on.

Rachel was now going to work at Macy's in South Coast Plaza because of Macy's acquiring Bullocks. Our relationship had taken a new turn, and I embraced the responsibility that came with it. It was a feeling I had never experienced before, but it felt right like I had found my anchor in life. It was as if a guardian instinct had awakened within me, and I was determined to protect her and provide her with the best life possible. The depth of my feelings for her was uncharted territory, and I welcomed this new aspect of myself with open arms.

As my last day at Continental Graphics approached, my coworkers threw me a heartfelt going-away party. We celebrated at a club, and though it started with joyous toasts, the drinks flowed freely, leading to a tipsy return to work. Amidst the merry atmosphere, I bid farewell to my Filipino colleague, parting ways with a picture she had given me long ago. It was the only picture I had of her, but I did not want to see it or her again. It was a symbolic gesture of closure, as I was ready to embrace the changes ahead.

And so, my journey at Continental Graphics came to an end. A new chapter was about to unfold as I ventured into a fresh start in Orange County with Rachel by my side. The following weeks were filled with excitement and a hint of nervousness as Rachel and I prepared for the move. Little did I know that this was only the beginning of the beautiful things ahead, for we were not just moving locations; we were stepping into a future full of love, growth, and endless possibilities. As we set forth on this path of new beginnings, I held tight to the belief that a greater plan was guiding us, just as the LORD had promised.

As I stepped into Arcade, Inc., an import/export company dealing in luxury furniture, it brought fresh challenges and opportunities. The responsibilities were greater, and the atmosphere felt invigorating. I was determined to excel in this role and prove my worth. As for Rachel, she quickly adapted to her new workplace at South Coast Plaza, and her resilience and hard work earned her respect among her colleagues. Our journey together in Orange County began a new chapter in our lives. With each passing day, our love and commitment deepened, and the belief that there was a divine plan for us took root in our hearts.

Arcade Inc. was a small startup company with only two of us, the owner and me, and I held the role of Operations Manager. From shipping and receiving clerk to forklift driver, receptionist to packer, mail clerk, and everything in between, I enthusiastically embraced each responsibility. My pay was $8 per hour, a dollar more than what I earned at my previous job at Continental Graphics, but I felt content with it.

Life moved swiftly, and as Christmas approached, I shared with Rachel my idea of eloping in Las Vegas. The urgency surprised her, but she agreed. On December 25, 1994, we tied the knot in Las Vegas, with two kind strangers acting as witnesses. Our stay at the Hacienda Hotel holds fond memories, although the Mandalay Bay Resort has now replaced the hotel.

"He who finds a wife finds what is good and receives favor from the Lord." Proverbs 18:22

In January 1995, we signed a lease for a one-bedroom condo near South Coast Plaza in Costa Mesa, paying $700 monthly. Rachel worked at Macy's, and we were barely making ends meet. I still recall the time when we ran out of money and food. Hope was scarce until, one day, a glimmer of luck came our way. I had bought a lottery ticket earlier, and when we checked it, we had won $70! Ecstatic and grateful, we rushed to the grocery store and filled our cart with much-needed groceries.

But life's twists and turns had something else in store for us. On a rainy day, as we left the supermarket, a speeding car appeared out of nowhere, colliding with several other vehicles and eventually hitting us from the driver's side. My car spun like a merry-go-round, but the reckless driver showed no signs of stopping. The crash left Rachel and me shaken and in shock. Concerned passersby rushed to our aid, and we found ourselves in a daze, contemplating what had just happened.

Thankfully, we weren't severely injured, but we needed assistance. An ambulance arrived, and though we didn't require hospitalization, we received medical attention at the scene. Rachel suffered a broken collar bone, and we both had severe whiplash. The police arrived and asked if I could identify the car that hit us. Riding along with them, we tracked down the culprit's residence, but to our surprise, we found him inside the vehicle, having taken his own life. Shocked and bewildered, we learned his wife and children were inside the house when he did it. Furthermore, the man was an off-duty police officer.

This incident left us emotionally scarred, but life continued. I returned to work, but the accident left my car totaled. Fortunately, the insurance company paid for the outstanding balance, but we still needed a new vehicle. The owner of Arcade Inc. offered to sell us one of his cars, a 1992 Mitsubishi Mirage hatchback, which we fondly named "The Chariot."

As I juggled work and life, the workload became overwhelming at Arcade. Hoping for some assistance, I convinced the owner to hire a young man named Fabio Gomes from Brazil, who was just passing through. He was actually on his way to Australia, where he aimed to surf. Inspired by his determination, I encouraged him, saying, "Where there is a will, there is a way." Fabio moved on, leaving behind his aspirations as I continued working.

However, I realized things weren't changing much at Arcade and that I needed a fresh start. Seeking new opportunities, I landed an interview at Wiz Technology, Inc. in San Juan Capistrano, CA. They offered me a shipping and receiving clerk job for $8.50 per hour, but I negotiated for $9.00 per hour before accepting the offer.

And so, a new chapter in my life began at Wiz Technology, a high-tech company dealing in internet applications and low-cost computer software products. Little did I know that this change would lead to even greater transformations.

It was another day at work, and as usual, I was busy trying to keep up with the flood of orders being shipped out. My hands were sore and blistered from keying in information, scanning, and labeling around 700 to 800 orders daily. During my work, the O.J. Simpson verdict was being read on the only TV in the warehouse. The executives gathered around, and when the "not guilty" verdict was announced, I couldn't contain my relief and blurted out a loud "YES!" But my reaction didn't go over well with everyone, and I was told to be cautious not to upset the front office.

Time passed, and after working there for six months, news broke that the Purchasing Manager was resigning, leaving a vacancy to be filled. When they asked if anyone had purchasing experience, I eagerly volunteered and expressed interest in the position. To my delight, I was granted an interview opportunity. I shared the news with Rachel, and we prayed about it together. The interview went well, and a week later, the HR Manager called me to her office with good news. They offered me the position of Purchasing Manager, but there was a catch – I would be on probation for the first six months, and the pay was $10.00 per hour.

Though I had hoped for a higher salary, I accepted the offer because it meant moving away from the warehouse job and seeing the growth potential. As the new Purchasing Manager, I was also the buyer and the purchasing clerk, but I was content with my title. One day, as I delved into the company's expenses, I noticed that we were purchasing CDs at a staggering cost of around $0.70 per CD, which included games and printing. Curious, I decided to check the market and reached out to companies like Sony and JVC Disc. Shockingly, Sony offered to sell CDs at just $0.10 each, and JVC cost was $0.12 for orders over ten thousand. Other companies' bids ranged from $0.12 to $0.15 per CD. This discovery puzzled me as to why we were paying so much more.

Armed with this information, I decided to discuss the matter with my boss, the COO, Mr. G. He was equally astonished by the price difference and asked me to leave the offers with him to investigate further. The consequences of my findings were dramatic – there was yelling, door slamming, and people leaving the company, including the CFO. Despite the turmoil, the COO instructed me to cancel open Purchase Orders and postpone placing new ones. He arranged a meeting with the current CD vendor, and I was asked to attend.

During the meeting, the vendor did not recognize me when they entered the conference room. They began disparaging remarks about the "Cason guy" and cracking inappropriate jokes, assuming I was Jewish. Unbeknownst to them, I was, in fact, Cedric Cason. When the COO revealed my identity, their faces turned pale, and the meeting proceeded in an awkward silence.

After this eye-opening encounter, we cut ties with the overpriced vendor and swiftly removed our inventory. The COO was impressed with my actions, and as a reward, he handed me a set of keys and announced that I was being given a company car for my exemplary work. I was overjoyed as I had never imagined such recognition. The HR Manager offered me another offer not long after – a salary position with full medical and dental coverage, earning $40,000 per year. My excitement soared even higher, and when she handed me a company credit card for expenses related to the company car, I was on cloud nine.

The company car I received was a brand new 1994 Jeep Grand Cherokee that had belonged to a departing employee. I rushed to show Rachel our amazing new vehicle; she was equally amazed and grateful. We celebrated this blessing with a trip to the car wash and a nice dinner, and back at home, we thanked the Lord for guiding us through this incredible journey of change and success.

Chapter 20: The Wiz Tech Run

(New Home, Wedding in Nairobi, Kenya, Farewell Wiz Technology)

It didn't take me long to settle into my new position at Wiz Technology as the Purchasing Manager. Mr. G., the Chief Operations Officer (COO), took me under his wing, and because of that, I received special treatment from his side. He often invited Rachel and me over to his lavish home situated in a beautiful, gated community in Dana Point, California. There, we got a glimpse of how the "rich" people lived; I was surprised to discover that they were no different than the rest of us peasants.

Mr. G and his girlfriend Becky were very down-to-earth and welcoming folks. We enjoyed spending time with them, and they also enjoyed our company. They liked Rachel and found it interesting that she was born and bred in Nairobi, Kenya. Mr. G started teaching me how to feel like I belonged, which taught me to believe in myself and feel that I belonged wherever I was, even if it meant hanging out and around millionaires.

I appreciated Mr. G inviting us to come over and watch the Mike Tyson fights over his house on fight nights. The food was amazing, and all his wealthy friends would be there. We would have a blast even though the fights were very short because of Mike Tyson's knockouts, which meant the fight night turned into poker night.

One thing I will never forget that Mr. G told me, "If you want to be successful, then surround yourself with successful people, and if you want to be smarter, then surround yourself with people that are smarter than yourself," and just the opposite, "If you want to be negative about everything, then surround yourself around negative people, and before you know it, you will be complaining about everything," he paused, before continuing, "If you want to be a drug addict, then surround yourself with people that do drugs." Basically, be around the people who you strive to be – lesson learned.

As things were going smoothly at Wiz Technology, my previous supervisor, the warehouse manager, left the company for reasons unknown to me. But soon after he left, they offered me the chance to take over his position. This meant that I was the new Operations Manager/Purchasing Manager. Now, I had developed a small Purchasing Department, but I would have to manage the warehouse operation that consisted of a staff of about 47 individuals. I took the opportunity and ran with it.

Within the first six months, I rearranged the entire warehouse, setting up security cages to reduce the amount of pilfering, separated the receiving dock from the shipping to improve productivity, and created a new procedure for our semi-annual inventories. The front office, including Mr. G, was very impressed. With my first management job after being in the Marine Corps for 12 years, this was a piece of cake.

Wiz Technology was continuing to grow as a company, and some investors needed continuous growth. In March 1996, the CEO of DSR, a big enterprise from New York, was arriving to meet with the executive staff and tour our facility. Therefore, my staff and I worked our tail off, preparing the entire facility. We were eagerly waiting for the CEO while a man sat in the reception area. As I was on my way to the receptionist's desk, I heard the name 'Willie Woods,' who paged for a call. As the call came out, the CFO, Billie Jolson, the one caught taking bribes from our old CD vendor, came out of her office looking for Willie Woods. I guessed at that time Willie Woods must have been the name of the CEO we were expecting from DSR.

Billie Jolson looked into the receptionist area and saw a black man sitting there. As I was approaching the reception area, she stared at me and stated, "That Willie Woods could not be here" because the only man she saw in the reception area was a black man. I looked at her and said, "Excuse me?" She again stated that Willie Woods was the CEO of DSR and the man in the reception, therefore, could not be him. She made sure that the receptionist and I, who also was black, heard what she had said. I could not believe what I had just heard and stood there in disbelief while Makeda, the receptionist, said in a loud voice, "And why not?" At the same time, the black man walked to the receptionist's desk and stated that he was Willie Woods and asked Makeda for the line number his call was on. I was still in shock at what I had just heard, and then Billie Jolson came out of her office again, realizing that the guy at the receptionist's desk was, indeed, Willie Woods.

I couldn't believe that this woman had the audacity to look at Makeda and me and give us two thumbs up, suggesting that a member of a minority finally made it to the top. I was boiling over with anger and frustration, but I kept my cool in front of Mr. Willie Woods. After the meeting was over and Mr. Willie Woods left the premises, I spoke to Makeda and told her that I was filing a formal complaint against our CFO, Billie Olson, and suggested that she do the same. After we filed formal complaints to the President, CEO, and Mr. G, the COO, within a week, Billie Jolson was no longer working at the company's office. We thought she got fired but later to find out that she was still working as the CFO and was instructed to work from home.

I started to wonder what she had on the owners to have that much power. I asked Mr. G about it, but he didn't utter a word. He just told me to keep my head down and focus on the job, but I could tell he was irritated as hell because he was the one who confronted her about taking kickbacks from our vendors. This was my first experience of blatant racism since I left the Marine Corps, and it was a learning experience for me outside of the Military. I realized that regardless of military or civilian life, racism or hatred was everywhere.

Meanwhile, Rachel and I were still settling in and preparing to let our friends know we had eloped. After hearing the news, everyone was pleased to hear that we had tied the knot. My old neighbors from San Diego, Rodney, and Lisa, had moved back to the Bay Area after Rodney was honorably discharged from the Navy.

I always stayed in touch with them because Rodney and I became close friends – they were just good people. On top of that, they were an excellent couple. Like if you look in the dictionary for a perfect married couple, you will see a picture of Rodney and Lisa. I had introduced them to other girlfriends before but wanted them to meet Rachel. So, I invited them to Costa Mesa for the weekend.

Rodney and Lisa loved meeting Rachel, and Lisa and Rachel hit it off very well. As time passed, Rachel expressed that she wanted to have our wedding in Nairobi and that that would be the only way her parents would accept our marriage. So, we did not tell anyone in Nairobi about our marriage; we just notified them of our intentions to get married there.

In June of 1996, Rachel and I set a wedding date of October 11, 1997, to get married in Nairobi, Kenya. We sent out the invitations, and all our family and friends were excited and happy for us. I asked Rodney if he would be my best man at our wedding, and he accepted. To my surprise, my parents, Eddie and Gloria Anderson, were all in from the beginning and stated that they planned on traveling to Kenya to be a part of our wedding. I was pleasantly surprised as they just had broken ground on building their custom home for their retirement and coming to our wedding meant they would not be present for some of the construction. But they came anyway.

Meanwhile, we considered purchasing our first home but did not believe we would qualify. An old friend of mine from the Marine Corps, Dawud Akil, who had always been an entrepreneur since I met him, convinced Rachel and me that we would qualify, and we did. Therefore, we purchased our first home in Corona, California 1996. After settling into our new home, we set off to Nairobi, Kenya, for our wedding.

My parents, Rodney and Lisa, came and were a part of the wedding. My parents and I were on the same boat with the Kenyan Kikuyu wedding traditions. Therefore, they participated in all the pre-wedding meetings with Rachel's family and the negotiation of the dowry. It got intense at times, but somehow, we all got through it. Then came the best day of our lives - On October 11, 1997, we were married by Bishop Peter Njenga at the beautiful Nairobi Cathedral in Nairobi, Kenya.

After the wedding, I learned everything back at Wiz Tech was going well. I never accepted kickbacks from vendors and never would. They own you once you accept a bribery or a kickback from a vendor. Even after Billie Jolson got caught accepting kickbacks, ripping off the company, and making racist remarks in the workplace, she was still employed as an officer of the company. Maybe it was because I was told that Billy Jolson was either the grandchild or the great-grandchild of the Great Al Jolson. I guess the apple does not fall far from the tree. But what I did learn from successful companies and owners is that they watch each other's backs. They take care of each other by sharing the fruits of their labor. For instance, they invited each other to their luxury suites at professional sporting events, such as luxury golf outings, yacht sailing, etc. I guess it is not kickbacks when you are signing the checks.

After a while, they started to ask me to attend these types of recreations when they were busy, or they did not want to but did not want to upset their business partners. Therefore, I attended San Diego Chargers and Padres games in luxury boxes. Luxury seating at Lakers and Clipper games, luxury golf outings, etc. I remember Mr. G got a call to play golf one afternoon at Pelican Hill Golf Resort in Newport Beach, CA. He immediately called me and asked if I played golf, and, of course, I said yes. He asked me if I did not mind taking the afternoon off to go play golf with one of the company's business partners, to which I agreed.

I had never played golf at the country club level. When I pulled up, a gentleman came and opened the door before I could even get out of my car. Before I knew it, someone had opened my trunk before I knew it, and another gentleman was taking my golf clubs from it. He also grabbed my golf shoes - I stopped him and said that I needed my shoes. He looked at me, smiled, and told me that my shoes would be on the cart with my clubs after they had been polished. I was blown away by the service given to me at Pelican Hill Golf Resort. I did not experience any racism there - everything was good. But now I understood what Mr. G meant when he said those words of wisdom to me. From that day forward, I belonged wherever I went.

After the round of golf, I realized that I had to enhance my game if I wanted to play at that level again. The next thing I knew, I was at the San Diego Charger training camp in San Diego, having lunch with Bobby Ross, the head coach at the time, and Junior Seau. I was in total awe and very nervous. So, I struck up a conversation with Junior Seau. I asked him if he was looking forward to the season beginning and asked if he was a hundred percent healthy. Junior Seau smiled at me and said, "No one is a hundred percent healthy in the NFL, but you play anyway because you love the game." Then I turned and looked at Bobby Ross, and he just looked at me with a straight face. Before that day was over, I had, and still have to this day, an autographed NFL football signed by all of the San Diego

Chargers Hall of Famers and other sports memorabilia from them.

Later that year, I remember being at a Charger game with seats in a luxury box. The owner got upset at me because he came in and saw me watching the St. Louis Cardinal playoff baseball game on a TV in his luxury suite. It was the playoffs, and I am a St. Louis Cardinal fan for life – it was obvious. Needless to say, I was not invited back to the luxury box.

One Friday, Mr. G asked me and another person at Wiz Technology if we knew a band called the Monkeys, and of course, I said yes. I grew up watching the Monkeys on TV. He said he had tickets to the show that weekend and asked if we wanted to go to Laughlin with him to see the show. I called Rachel to see if she was cool with me hanging out with Mr. G. that weekend to go see the Monkeys. She said, "Yes, go for it."

Therefore, the three of us were speeding to Laughlin in Mr. G's brand new S600 Mercedes Benz, going around 120 miles per hour. He also had a business meeting, so this was kind of like a business trip. All I remember is that by the end of the night, Davy Jones and I were hanging out at the bar, wasted, laughing, and having a great time. When one of the Monkeys, Micky Dolenz, came and told us that was enough, he asked Davy Jones to finish up so he could take him back to the room. I remember Micky Dolenz telling me how funny it is that times had changed because when they were younger, Davy Jones came to get Dolenz after a night of drinking. They left, but that whole evening was wild.

Back at Wiz Technology, the company was moving forward with a new vision that was presented to management. We were presented with the idea of Wiz Technology becoming the first company that offered internet e-commerce, and that new branch would be named 'Cappo Tech.' It was indeed a fact that before Amazon hit the big screen, this small, publicly owned computer software company located in San Juan Capistrano, CA, was to launch an interactive, online e-commerce company where anyone could shop at their favorite department stores or any other store by the tip of their fingertips.

Within the following months, they hired new management, such as IT Manager, Web Manager, and Marketing Manager, with a handful of software programmers. We were all excited – business was booming, and the price of our shares was increasing, which made our annual bonuses more valuable. We received not only cash bonuses but also stock options.

I was still the Operations/Purchasing Manager, managing the purchasing department and also the warehouse/distribution center. I remember one of my best employees in the warehouse, who I had hired to do my first job at the company - shipping and receiving clerk. His name was Manuel Beltran - a young Hispanic male who looked like he wanted to be a gang member. However, I did not look at him that way. He wanted to look the part and act the part, but there was something more about Manuel that I saw in him.

Mr. Beltran would check in late often and missed a lot of days, but he was my best shipping and receiving clerk. I did not have to worry about shipping and receiving when he was there. Sometimes, he would miss multiple days at a time and assume that he was fired. And when he called in, I would always ask him how soon I could expect him to get here, and then an hour later, he would roll up and get to work. He reminded me of myself when I was young and in the Marine Corps, getting in trouble. But people like Gunny Hunt and Gunny Colon would always believe in second chances. So, I gave forward and gave multiple chances to Manuel. Mr. G. and I became friends with him.

While working at Wiz Technology, Mr. G. got engaged to his girlfriend, Becky. He asked me to be a part of his wedding. I was blown away. So, Rachel and I attended Mr. G's wedding in Las Vegas. Mr. G was Italian and looked like he was in the movie Goodfellas. Anyway, I was the only black person in the groomsmen group. And when we took a picture, it looked like we were the Rat Pack.

Suddenly, at Wiz Technology, things got weird. A lot of closed-door meetings were happening. Mr. G was not a part of these meetings, and you could tell that he was uncomfortable with the situation. I heard all kinds of rumors, but nothing tangible. All of a sudden, Mr. G resigned from the company, and I was in shock. I asked Mr. G what had happened, and he just said he did not like being kept in the dark and would not be part of an organization if he was not part of the decision-making process. Mr. G was an officer of the company and owned at least a quarter of the shares, and yet they kept him out. Mr. G told me to keep my head down, just keep doing my job, and that I should not have anything to worry about.

Within a year, we had lost over half of our employees, and layoffs were inevitable. Before you knew it, I was called into the executive office and was told I would have to lay off around 90% of the remaining staff. I was in shock, thinking I must be next. But, even on that same day, which was payday, people were returning from the bank, stating that the bank would not cash their checks because there were not enough funds in their accounts. The owner had to go and make a deposit so employees could cash their checks.

The next week was the worst week in my career as a manager. I had to hand out layoff notifications to 90% of our employees, from the front office to the warehouse. It was horrible, and people were infuriated – rightfully so.

I remember the last month before I put in my resignation - no one was there. I sat in my office with the door closed, spending all day faxing my resume to every fax number I could find in the wanted section. Rachel and I had just purchased our first home, and we had a mortgage to pay. I remember praying in my office, asking GOD to help me find a new position at the same level that I was currently in. I was not about to start looking for hourly jobs that paid minimum wage. Mr. G had taught me that I belonged, and at this point in my life, I felt that there was no job that I could not do in the field of Procurement and/or Warehouse Operations Management. I did not care what position they were looking for - if I found a fax number, I sent my resume.

I finally got a call from an HR Manager at a company called Starcrest Products of California, located in Perris, CA. The HR Manager stated they were interested in filling a Purchasing Manager position and asked if I would like to come in for an interview. I accepted the interview. The interview with the HR Manager went well. I eventually got the call back for a second interview with the Services Manager, and I thought that could have gone either way, but I remained optimistic.

GOD answered my prayer. Lo and behold, about a couple of weeks later, they called me to make me a job offer, but the salary was way lower than my current salary, which was a little over $$55,000 annually. They lowballed me, but I was not in a position to be picky. I negotiated a little higher than they were offering, but I also asked the HR Manager if she would put in my contract that if I proved myself within the first six months, I would be eligible for a substantial pay increase in salary. She agreed to include that in my contract.

The following Monday at Wiz Technology, I asked for a meeting with the President and the CEO, the President's wife. I submitted my resignation to the President and gave a 30-day notification. Immediately, the CEO asked for the keys to the Jeep, my company car. I was thinking, *'Really? After I caught the CFO ripping off the company for more than $150,000 a year, you going to ask for this petty jeep back? Really?'* The amount of money I saved for this company was more than double my salary. I stated that the company's car was part of my salary, and if she wanted the keys back, they should pay me that part of my salary back in cash. She got very upset, but the President asked his secretary how much the company still owed on the Jeep. She came back with an estimate of $10 thousand. The President said, "I will make you a deal - if you pay off the balance of the jeep, you can keep the jeep." So, I went out and got a loan for $10 thousand and kept the jeep.

Friday, March 27, 1998, was my last day at Wiz Technology. Three days later, Monday, March 30, 1998, was my first day at Starcrest Products of California as their new Purchasing Manager. I later found out that 30 days after I left Wiz Technology, the Orange County Sheriff's Deputies came and put locks on the doors and that Wiz Technology had filed for bankruptcy.

Me and Davy Jones from the Monkey.

Magic Johnson and I.

Chapter 21: Starcrest Products, Positions and Highlights, Friends We Lost, Resigning

A wave of memories pours in as I reflect on my time at Starcrest Products of California - a mosaic of encounters, difficulties, friendships, and events that have influenced my life. Situated in the heart of Costa Mesa, California, Starcrest, a business that started out in 1973 as a mail-order company selling a single line of pantyhose, became more to me than just a place to work; it was an era of my life that was full of development, solidarity, and unanticipated turns. The current CEO and his father founded Starcrest Products, which is now headquartered in Perris, California. Meanwhile, the company offers a wide range of products, including kitchenware, clothing, health and beauty products, etc., with around 8,000 active items.

When I started at Starcrest Products of California, the company was one of the largest mail-order companies in the country, with over 1,000 employees. The marketed product catalog had five distinct divisions: Starcrest Products of California, Signatures, Handsome Rewards, Make Life Easier, and Gavilan's. I spent 15 years at Starcrest in four different management positions: Purchasing Manager (5 years and 10 months), Quality Manager (2 years and four months), Production Control Manager (4 years and 11 months), and switchboard manager (2 years and four months). Starcrest is more than just a job; it has become a family. I put blood, sweat, and tears into this company and have grown tremendously as a manager.

***

Just a quick update about Wiz Technology: After a year with Starcrest, I got the following notification from Mr. G, my old boss at Wiz Technology: It stated:

"Litigation Release No. 16298 / September 28, 1999

The Securities and Exchange Commission announced today that it has sued the three top officers of WIZ Technology, Inc., headquartered in San Juan Capistrano, CA, for financial fraud and insider trading. The Complaint alleges that the three used accounting gimmicks, sham sales, and backdated agreements artificially to inflate WIZ's publicly reported sales, income, assets, etc.

The Commission sued the President, the Chief Executive Officer, and Billie Jolson, WIZ's former Chief Financial Officer."

Wow! I wasn't expecting it, but I wasn't shocked either.

***

During my time at Starcrest, one thing that struck me was the company's dedication to the management team. That is what I liked about Starcrest: that they invested in their management. Starcrest created an internal Management Academy that lasted just over a year and required all management to attend and graduate. It was evidence of the company's dedication to developing leadership abilities, encouraging growth, and ensuring its management team was prepared to sail the ship through turbulent seas.

However, not all of my experience at Starcrest was without difficulties. A negative thing about Starcrest for me was the high turnover rate for hourly employees. This turnover rate not only disrupted the stability of the workforce but also posed challenges to maintaining productivity levels. Additionally, it put a strain on the company's resources, as constant recruitment and training became necessary to fill vacant positions. Despite the teamwork among the management, this problem served as a constant reminder of the challenging circumstances many employees had to deal with. I cannot get into all my experiences at Starcrest; that will have to be another book, but after working for a company for over 15 years, you build relationships, some of which will last a lifetime.

Being a first-generation company, Starcrest had firmly established itself in the ways of the past. For instance, all management had to wear a collared shirt and a tie, regardless of the nature of their job. It made no difference if you were operating a forklift in temperatures of 100 degrees or working near conveyer belts; you had to wear a tie. I truly liked the owner because he was friendly and straightforward. You could just stroll into his office if you needed to speak with him, and he would take the time to hear your issues. The owner used to invite me to some of his equestrian competitions in San Juan Capistrano. I would go along with our son and enjoy the day.

Again, similar to what I accomplished at Wiz Technology, I reduced annual costs at Starcrest much more than my salary. We had outgrown our warehouse and were now using a facility off-site in a different city. These shipping containers, leased from Starcrest Products, were used to transport goods on cargo ships. Because we needed that cubic area to store goods close to the Distribution Center, we must have been renting about 300 trailers placed in the back of the warehouse. At that time, we were delivering an average of over 35,000 orders daily, each containing an average of three to four items. As a result, we had to rent containers to store products to keep them close to the picking line. Our monthly rent for each container ranged from $60 to $100 with the firm we were renting from. I was furious about this since, even though we had repeatedly paid for these containers, we were still renting them. When I asked about simply buying the containers, the owner responded that we weren't in the container business. So, I set out on a quest to renegotiate the container leasing agreement because I was determined to eliminate unnecessary expenses.

After talking with the owner about six months later, I called the firm from which we rented the containers and instructed them to start making plans to pick them up. The owner of the container firm called me right away to find out what was going on, and I explained that since we had already paid for the containers, they should have been our property by this point. Since they were unable to accept a significant reduction, we were going to start renting from another company. Obviously, I made up everything. I couldn't imagine us spending, on average, $70 a month for 300 containers, so I didn't care. This amounted to about $252,000 per year for cube space. I was asked to wait by the owner of the container company before we began bringing in additional containers.

The following day, he called and offered me $50 per container. I refused, saying that they belonged to us since we had already paid for the containers. He countered with $35 dollars per container with a year's lease, and I offered $20 per container as my offer. I informed him that I would have to discuss this with the owner because I knew we would not be getting rid of these containers any time soon. I notified my boss and my boss told the owner, who was astounded by the price reduction.

The owner literally stood up as my boss, and I were standing in his office with the approval to make the transaction for $35 dollars per container with a one-year minimum, looked at my boss, and said to him, "Good Job!"

Seriously? I could not believe it. The owner thanked my boss, yet my boss said nothing when I secured $132,000 in annual cost savings. He did not even utter a single word of gratitude.

For a brief moment, I was furious, but I was happy with the way the cost reductions turned out. I offered further recommendations that significantly reduced costs but never received praise for them. For instance, it took me two years to persuade Distribution Management and the executive staff that we should invest $22,000 in a trash compactor and reduce our trash pickup to twice a month instead of dumping our trash in containers and having three pickups a day, saving us $75,000 annually. The return on investment was less than three months. Go figure! Only if companies would utilize the Procurement Department seriously! Corporations should take note that "there should always be a spot at the table for a procurement professional within your organization."

It was a bittersweet victory that served as a reminder of the value that a devoted procurement professional can bring to a company's bottom line.

I remember one time in 15 years when the owner came to my office and warned me about people signing Purchase Orders and told me not to let it happen again. Yes, at Wiz Technology, I was signing million-dollar blanket Purchase Orders, but here, I could not even sign a five-dollar purchase order. Although I mentioned that this was a first-generation business, I also think they had extensive financial control measures in place because they had been burned in the past.

As a result, I had a secretary, clerks, junior buyers, and senior buyers under me as the purchasing manager. One of my Senior Buyers was an older gentleman whom I knew was overqualified when I hired him, but I hired him anyway because we were short on staff. Nevertheless, the Senior Buyer detested the fact that he lacked any authority to sign purchase orders, but one time, he could not help himself and did so. When the company's owner found out, it didn't take him long to come straight to my office to discuss the authority. He was furious when he mentioned that he was the only one with that authority and that if anyone signed the purchase order again, someone could lose their job.

As soon as he went out of my office, I called the Senior Buyer into my office and asked him, "What the hell were you thinking?"

The aftermath of this confrontation pushed me to the brink of losing my temper—a rarity for me as a manager. This was the only time I remember losing my patience as a manager because I remember saying out of anger, "Got damn it! If this happens again, I will walk you out myself!"

Right after the, Senior Buyer left my office, he went back to his cubicle, started to pack his stuff, and in a few moments, he walked out of the office. I was calm about the whole situation that unfolded before me because I was not going to allow a Senior buyer to lead me to lose my job.

After about an hour, my boss came into my office and asked me to follow him to the Human Resources Manager's Office. The expression on my boss' face was not pleasant, and he low-key mentioned something about how I was in trouble and that I needed to be really careful about what I said when we got into the HR Manager's Office.

As soon as we entered the HR Manager's office, she informed me that a worker had lodged a grievance against me and that he had resigned and left the building. I described what the employee did and how the company's owner had warned me about the negligence that took place in my department.

The HR manager stated that the employee was shocked by the language I used when speaking to him, and he was extremely disappointed in me because he knew from prior conversations that I was a Christian without showing any emotion. After a brief period of silence in the HR Manager's office, my boss asked, "Do you have anything to say?"

The HR Manager was waiting for my response. I took a moment to think before saying, "Yes, he knew that I was a Christian, but I forgot to tell him that I was Baptist."

They both looked at me, then at each other, and said I could go now. I never heard from my boss or the Human Resources Manager about the incident again.

***

I always copied the management style of my first manager, Mark Gray, from Continental Graphics. Mark was the calmest and nicest manager I have ever worked with, and he never lost his temper. I felt disappointed and vowed I would never let anyone upset me again. It was a lesson in maintaining professionalism, even when faced with challenges that test one's limits.

My journey at Starcrest was interconnected with personal relationships that spanned beyond office hours. I made deep connections with colleagues, some of whom became lifelong friends. You eventually, one way or another, lose the people you meet along the way. For instance, a group of us managers ate lunch together in the lunchroom daily. Our Customer Service Manager, Alan Walters, was the healthiest person I have ever met when it comes to nutrition and diet. Alan only ate healthy foods and participated in food research experiments. One day, Alan mentioned that his daughter was getting married soon, and he wanted to fly to Denver and get something very precious as a gift for the family, and he wanted to give it to his daughter for her wedding.

I, therefore, offered him one of Rachel's buddy passes since she had returned to her position as a flight attendant. When I offered him the buddy pass, Alan Walters accepted, flying to Denver the following weekend and flying back the following Sunday. He was supposed to join us for lunch on Monday, so we were curious as to why he was not there. We learned the following day that Alan had died on Monday as a result of an aneurysm he suffered while at the gym. Needless to say, we were all taken aback.

Cindy Whitaker, our training manager, was not only a colleague, but she and her husband Mitch were also good friends with us. They would visit our home for Christmas parties, and we would go to their home for barbecues. Cindy, who had recently been promoted to Human Resources Manager, was doing well.

At that time, I was the Production Control Manager. On a Tuesday morning, as soon as I arrived at work in the distribution center, Tracy Peak, an HR Supervisor who was also close with Cindy and her husband, called me. Tracy called me up in tears and delivered the very shocking news to me: "Cindy is gone."

I could not believe any word that I heard from Tracy and said, "What are you talking about? I just had a meeting with Cindy yesterday."

"Cindy and Mitch were in an accident, and Cindy did not make it." I could not believe Tracy when she described the incident to me until I looked up the local newspaper and read the report for myself. I cannot describe to you the pain I felt for weeks after losing Cindy. Everyone in the company was crying that day, and I found myself sobbing when I woke up in the middle of the night. It took me months to come to peace with the fact that Cindy Whitaker was gone. We were all heartbroken when Cindy passed away.

I got to know and gained some friendships for life, such as Mike Gibson, Carl Hodge, and Stan Roberts. Take our golfing group, for instance. There were five of us: James "Jim" Cagle, Andy Vallecorsa, Jack Carlisle, Tom Edmunds, and myself. We used to play a lot of golf on weekends when we were not working. But as life often reminds us, these bonds were not immune to the passage of time. The group was reduced from five to two over time due to tragedy, serving as a sobering reminder of the fleeting nature of life. Only Jim and I are left.

It all began when Jack Carlisle underwent back surgery and never returned from the hospital. After that, it was Andy. It was thought that Andy had died of cancer.

When I was working as the Telephone Order Center Manager at Starcrest, my friend Tom entered my office, shut the door quickly, and told me that he wanted to be the only one to inform me of this. Tom revealed to me that he had pancreatic cancer, would not undergo chemotherapy and that when the Lord called him home, he would be hitting golf balls with his Savior, Jesus Christ, from cloud to cloud. I was completely taken aback; Tom was a true friend, and I enjoyed hanging out and playing golf with him. Furthermore, Tom assured me that he would continue to work until he was admitted to hospice care. I did not comprehend why he would act in that manner, but I later learned it had to do with his insurance.

I watched hopelessly as Tom's cancer slowly consumed him over the course of the following six months. He frequently visited my office, and we had great conversations there. He eventually reached a point where he was unable to climb the stairs by himself and had to use the elevator. I would go downstairs to see Tom whenever he did not arrive because I assumed the elevator was out of service. I was dealing with personal issues that I did not share with Tom during his final days because I just wanted to be there for him.

My mother, Gloria Anderson, informed me that she had pancreatic cancer while I was watching Tom deteriorate in front of my eyes. I could not comprehend that fact and found it incomprehensible that my mother would experience what Tom was going through. Tom was a walking skeleton with a big smile in my office when I last saw him alive. He had lost all sense of taste and carried tennis balls with him to place under his legs when he sat.

The next day, I was notified that Tom was not strong enough to come to work. As I mentioned before, I was going through some serious personal issues myself, and I had seen enough. After I got the call regarding Tom, I called Rachel and could not say anything, and Rachel said, "Come home."

I told Rachel, "I can't do this job anymore; I need to get away."

She repeated her words with a hopeful voice: "Just come home; we have started over before, and we can do it again."

It did not take me long to start packing my belongings in a box right after I hung up the phone. Another manager came to my office and asked me, "What are you doing?"

"I am leaving, and I have to get out of here."

That was all I could say before my boss came into my office looking for the next quarter's forecasts and asked the same question as the manager, "What are you doing?"

"I have decided to leave the company," was all I said, and she could not believe it.

I finished packing my personal belongings while they watched, and by this time, the entire department was watching me in my office while I packed. I waved goodbye to my department as I was leaving because I did not want to start saying goodbyes. As I was waving, I noticed some of them were in tears, but I had to go. I, therefore, owed it to the owner to inform him of my departure as I was leaving the building. When I went into his office, he immediately noticed that I was carrying a box and assumed that I was leaving. He asked me, "So, Cedric, this is it?"

I responded with a very professional answer: "Yes, Sir, and I just wanted to thank you for the opportunity you gave me for the last fifteen years, but it is time for me to go."

In return, he asked me, "What are you going to do?"

"I have no idea, but I have to go," I said casually.

As I was leaving, he said, "If you ever want to return, the door will always be open."

I sincerely appreciated him before exiting and leaving to go home in my car. Tom Passed away on March 5, 2013. There is a ton more I could say about Starcrest Products of California, but once more, that would require a separate book.

Tom Edmunds and I playing golf 2012.

Chapter 22: Personal Life While At Starcrest Products, Honeymoon, and Meeting My Father's Family for the First Time

My personal life was bringing me surprises and changes that I could not have anticipated, but in a good way, when working at Starcrest. While Rachel and I were residing in Corona, California, she had recently received the "Employee of the Year" award from Macy's in South Coast Plaza, Costa Mesa, California. After that, she decided to return to her previous job as a flight attendant, which she had held with Pan Am until the airline went out of business.

Therefore, Rachel started working for United Airlines in July 1988, the same month I started working for Starcrest Products of California. My parents, who had both officially retired, visited us while we were still residing in Corona, California. Therefore, we decided to surprise both of them with a retirement party. We invited all of our San Diego-based friends and cousins to the party. Our close friend Kamau Kenyatta traveled from San Diego with his entire jazz band and entertained our guests and my parents with two lengthy but full-of-entertainment jazz performances. Kamau and his band's performances completely blew them away.

In the year 2002, a lot of things happened, including our decision to sell and buy another home in Moreno Valley, which was only a ten-minute drive away from Starcrest Products. I finally got to spend time with my son, Nicholas Cason, who is now thirteen and resides in Pensacola, Florida, with his mother. So, it was agreed that Nicholas would come to California and spend the summer with us. I was incredibly excited and had activities for us to do together planned for the entire summer. Even though things did not go as planned, we managed to get through the summer. In the summer of 2002, while Nicholas was still living with us, we traveled to East St. Louis to honor my parents' 25th wedding anniversary. At the summer of 2002's end, Nicholas returned to Pensacola, FL.

The fact that Rachel and I at last decided to go on our honeymoon in 2002 was another memorable event. We decided to spend our honeymoon in a country in East Africa called Kenya, where we also got married.

Our first stop was the Norfolk Hotel in Nairobi, Kenya. After a few days there, our transportation showed up, and we were on our way to the Masai Mara, a journey that took us eight hours and a safari jeep.

At the Mara Safari Club, we stayed in a tented camp. The tents featured wooden floors, king-sized beds, bathrooms, electricity, and a front porch with views of a river teeming with hippopotamuses. A powerful electrical fence surrounded the tent camp for security. We could hear various kinds of animals outside the fence at night.

Every day, we embarked on a safari in the Masai Mara. We saw nearly every wild animal there was to see; it was breathtakingly beautiful, and some animal migration was still going on. There were lions, cheetahs, gazelles, wild boars, elephants, giraffes, monkeys, and many other animals. It was a once-in-a-lifetime experience. The main clubhouse hosted a show every night when we returned to the tented camp in the evening. After staying in the Masai Mara for three nights, we returned to the Jeep and returned to Nairobi. One night was all we spent in Nairobi, and then we were back in the jeep and on our way to the Mount Kenya Safari Club.

The Mount Kenya Safari Club is perched high on the slopes of the second-highest mountain in Africa, which crosses the equator. It has luxurious cottages and an elegant building surrounded by well-kept lawns and ornamental ponds. This was completely different from the tented camps back in the Masai Mara. We were lodging in a stunning one-bedroom villa with a vast living room and two enormous fireplaces.

Every night, when we arrived back, our fireplace was lit, and our pillows and remaining chocolates were back in the bed. Rachel and I spent the day horseback riding, going on mini safaris, and playing golf, which was my first time doing so with a caddy. Every evening, the Mount Kenya

Safari Club served a nine-course, elaborate dinner complete with entertainment. Dinner jackets were mandatory. Before leaving for the United States, we had the opportunity to visit Rachel's mother and father once we were back in Nairobi, along with the rest of her family.

When we arrived back in the United States at LAX, we grabbed our luggage and boarded a bus to the parking lot. As I attempted to exit the bus with luggage in my hands, the bus side doors closed quickly behind me, launching me into the air. I was in terrible pain when I hit the ground with my knees.

The bus driver opened the side door once more as I rolled over, and passengers behind me started getting off again. When I attempted to stand up, I could not do so due to my inability to move my legs. I was trying to understand why she shut the doors on me. I could sense that something was not right. Rachel was waiting for me to stand, but I could not stand on my feet. I told Rachel that something was really wrong because I could not move my legs. I could see Rachel was concerned about me because of her worried expressions. People kept stepping over me as they exited the bus without offering any assistance. I was unable to move, so I asked Rachel to dial 911 for assistance. The bus driver came out, looked around, climbed back on the bus, and drove away like nothing happened. Rachel and I were the only ones there, waiting for an ambulance.

When the ambulance arrived, they asked what had happened to me, and I quickly told them I could not move my legs. One of the paramedical staff cut my pants open to check my knees, but when I looked at my knees, I had none. I had no idea what had happened to my knees when they put me on a gurney and transported me to "Centinela Hospital Medical Center" in Inglewood. I asked Rachel if she could find a Kaiser Hospital nearby after being unimpressed by the outdated-looking hospital. One of the medical assistants overheard me talking to Rachel and mentioning that I was looking for a Kaiser Hospital. He then advised me to look out the window. Looking out the window, I saw a big sign that read, "Tommy Lasorda Sports Wing Orthopedic Specialist."

He continued by saying, "Since we work for the Lakers, Clippers, Kings, and Dodgers, we have the best orthopedic surgeons on the West Coast."

I responded, "I think we will stay here," as I turned to face Rachel.

He turned to face me and said, "I now have a question for you."

To which I replied, "What is it?"

He asked me if I had PPO insurance. If I did not, then I would have to go to Kaiser or a County Hospital.

I answered his question with, "Yes, I do have PPO Insurance."

In reply to the answer, he said, "Then you are in good hands."

Before a doctor entered the room, we remained there for another 30 minutes, approximately. The doctor informed us that he was leaving the parking lot and heading home when he received the page requesting his return to the hospital.

Dr. Chandran, M.D., was an Indian doctor specializing in total joint reconstruction and general orthopedics. The other medical assistant in the room gave me a quick glance before telling me that it was my lucky day. After confirming and approving my insurance, Dr. Chandran returned to the room and informed me that both of my patellar ligaments were fractured and disconnected. My patellas were now situated just below my upper thighs, which is why my knees were flat.

He stated that I would require an immediate operation and that my recovery would be lengthy. When he asked if I wanted the surgery immediately, I said, "Yes, sir."

You could tell Rachel was very worried from the expression on her face. I made a few jokes to try and make her laugh, but she was having none of it. She was terrified, and I was too, but I was not going to show it to her.

When Dr. Chandran returned, he said that although they were ready to take me into the operating room, he needed to ask me a question first. Dr. Chandran told me, "This is critical, and I need your honest response." So, he asked if I had previously participated in sports and if I planned to participate in sports in the future, and I answered that question with a "Yes."

To which Dr. Chandran replied, "Good, now we know how to proceed."

As they wheeled me into the operating room for my surgery, I asked Rachel to call Starcrest and inform them of my absence and what had happened. It was a Sunday afternoon, and the last question I asked the gentleman wheeling me into the operating room was,

"Do you know what the score of the Raiders game is?"

Ten hours later, my legs were completely cast from my high thigh to my toes when I woke up in a new hospital room in the most agonizing pain I had ever experienced in my life. I called for a nurse while groaning, and when one arrived, she instructed me to press the button in my hand to relieve the pain. It was a button for morphine release. I initially believed I had Carpal Tunnel Syndrome because I was pressing that button like I was playing a video game. For a few hours, the morphine would put me to sleep for good, and when I came back to my senses, I would start pressing the button once more. This lasted for roughly 24 hours, after which they began weaning me off the morphine and switching me to oxycodone.

After three days in the hospital, I was discharged and ready to return home. By the time Rachel contacted the insurance provider, a hospital bed had already been delivered to our residence and set up in my office on the first floor of our home. As a result, the hospital sent medical assistants to help Rachel put me in the car's back seat as she needed assistance, and then we were on our way home. I asked Rachel if she could call Starcrest on my behalf and let them know that I might require assistance getting out of the car and into my bed at home when I got home because I did not know how I would get out of it.

Two Starcrest managers were waiting to help us get me out of the car and into our house on the hospital bed when we got home, so they helped us do that. I clearly recall thinking,

"Why?" I asked God, "Why did this have to happen to me?" as I lay in my hospital bed at home for the first time.

I unexpectedly experienced a sense of calmness. God had to humble me; I needed to reconsider who I was and what I stood for. Going forward, I needed to remain humble and grateful for what I had taken for granted. I also needed to rest. I was told that I would have to wear the cast for at least six weeks, followed by four months of rehabilitation / physical therapy.

My parents flew out and stayed with us for a few weeks to give Rachel a break because she was working hard with me but was getting worn out and needed a break. After that, Rachel returned to her job. My father built a ramp for me in the backyard so that my wheelchair could roll down, and I could sit on the patio there. The ability to sit outside was pleasant.

Starcrest's executive team agreed to let me work from home to help me maintain a resemblance of a salary while my disability was nowhere in sight. Julian and Dawud, two of my old Marine Corps friends, came by to help me with day-to-day tasks.

After six weeks, we returned to Centinela Hospital Medical Center in Inglewood to have the casts removed. I was ecstatic until they removed the casts and revealed my legs. My legs were skinny with no muscle, and my skin was filthy and flaky with dead skin. Furthermore, when the casts were removed, I was unable to bend my knees. It was the same level of discomfort as when I woke up from my surgery. So they put these temporary casts on both of my legs so I could begin the process of attempting to bend my knees. So, I had to start physical therapy.

Physical therapy's first few days were absolute hell; the pain was so unbearable that I did not intend to return. My physical therapist asked if I was taking my medication, and I replied,

"What medication?"

She was surprised to learn that I was not taking any medication. She advised me to contact my surgeon about the medication as soon as possible. When I called Dr. Chandran, he said I should have been given prescriptions when I left the hospital, and I told him I did not get any prescriptions when I left the hospital. He was distraught and immediately wrote me a prescription. He asked that I go pick up the medication and reminded me that there was some medication I needed to take before my physical therapy.

I was able to endure the pain of physical therapy once I started taking the medication. I had a long way to go before I was actually able to walk again and bend my knees somewhat, which took me about three months. My legs never really regained their mass.

The surgery was successful, which was good news. In therapy, I came into contact with individuals who had water on the knee and had undergone a second or third surgery. Dr. Chandran responded in a very loud voice when I told him what had happened, saying,

"You have one time and one time only to get the surgery right. It will never be right if you do not get it right the first time. I spent five hours on both knees making sure I did it correctly the first time, which is why it took me so long."

Although it was a long journey, I was fortunate to be close to Centinela Hospital, and I was also very lucky that Dr. Chandran was still on site when he was contacted. Since I had two tours on the drill field and a Leadership Instructor job at NCO School in between the two tours, I will be honest and say that my knees were exhausted. I truly believe my knees are better now than before the surgery.

In 2004, my biological father invited me to their family reunion in Berkley, California. I was hesitant to go because I had never met anyone from my biological father's family outside of St. Louis, but Rachel thought it would be a good idea to meet that side of the family. So we decided to rent a convertible and drive up the California coast, stopping in Cambria, Monterey, and then Berkley for the Family Reunion. It was a pleasure driving up the coast; we visited Hurst Castle in Cambria and the Monterey Aquarium.

When we arrived in Berkeley and checked into the hotel, I saw the first people who looked like me. It was strange, and after waiting so long for my biological father to introduce me to his family, I felt betrayed. Two older gentlemen, resembling my father, approached me and asked my name. I introduced myself as Cedric Cason, which confused them because I did not share their surname. When they asked who my father was, I told them it was Leo Wofford. They exclaimed loudly that I resembled Leo but had no idea Leo had a son.

Both of these gentlemen were my uncles. My father was delighted to see me talking to his brothers. I told him that we would stay for the banquet and the Picnic, but then we would go to Stockton to see one of Rachel's friends and then to Napa Valley for a few days before returning home. So, while at the banquet, I met many people I had never met before, and my father was excited to introduce me to his family.

When it came time to discuss family history that had been passed down from our Great-Great Grandparents who were slaves, I noticed that almost all of my uncles were crying like babies. Then it dawned on me: This is why I cry so easily. So, on Sunday morning, it is customary for my father's family to hold a church service in one of the hotel's meeting rooms, and I decided to attend.

People rose to speak, and one of my aunts asked if I had anything to say to the family. I hesitated at first but eventually stood up and spoke up. I told them that,

"I hated my father, and I do not want anything to do with him or his family because I did not exist to him or you all. But, I have come to realize this weekend that I do have a family that I have never known, and my father was finally very excited to introduce me to everyone, so I have decided this morning that I will not carry any kind of hate for him anymore because it is only affecting me. I forgive as God forgives, and it was a pleasure meeting everyone this weekend."

When I looked at my father and his brothers, they were all sobbing like babies. It seems to run in the family. Rachel and I packed up the convertible after the service, said our goodbyes, and drove away. I have been to two more family reunions on my father's side since then, one in Seattle and one in St. Louis.

Chapter 23: A Journey of Faith and Purpose

My son, Isaac Franklin Cason, was born on a rainy Friday at 8:38 a.m., May 6, 2005, which marked a profound turning point in my life. The joy that welled up inside me on that day was immeasurable. As we welcomed Isaac into our family, I can clearly remember carrying him into our backyard, raising his tiny form cradled in my arms while I gazed up at the sky, raindrops splattering gently around us. Oh, the joy of being a father again and having that bundle of joy in my arms. It was clearly a blessing of God.

With Isaac held high, I offered a heartfelt prayer to God: "Isaac belongs to you. May he do great things, giving you all the Glory. Protect him, guide him, and use him to Glorify you." It was a sacred promise, a dedication of my son's future to a higher purpose.

Before Isaac was born, we purchased a home - the one that had become our haven and would be Isaac's sanctuary for the next eighteen years. However, as the initial euphoria of his birth gave way to everyday life, an ever-present shadow began to loom over me.

Anxiety had been lurking on the outskirts of my life like an unrelenting ghost. It became increasingly obvious over time, so much so that I could not carry its weight by myself. My wife, Rachel, gently prodded me in the direction of getting assistance out of concern for my well-being. I had not previously acknowledged my struggle with severe anxiety and depression, which I had been dealing with long before I quit my job at Starcrest Products of California.

At first, I resisted getting help from a professional. Stubbornly, I had brushed aside the notion that I needed help. I could not picture myself, a strong black man, having mental health problems. However, as the months turned into a relentless battle against my own mind, I gave in. I finally heeded Rachel's advice and sought out a psychiatrist. I am grateful to Rachel for pushing and encouraging me to go into therapy. It was also a true blessing that I had such a caring and supportive wife.

I started seeing a psychiatrist, and I opened up that I also had bouts of depression, and I didn't know why. Through months of therapy, my internal turmoil began to unfold. I realized that at the core of my anxiety was an unspoken, hidden fear - the fear of losing my family, Rachel and Isaac. It was a worry that I had suppressed for a long time, one so ingrained that it had negatively impacted my health without my knowledge. The fear of losing loved ones was something I had unfortunately experienced again and again.

My therapist and I traced this buried pain back to my time in the Marine Corps, a painful chapter I had long tried to forget. I vividly recall the demotion from Sergeant to Corporal, a professional setback that had fractured my family and led to the loss of a meaningful relationship with my daughter from that previous marriage. In those dark days, I had even wrestled with thoughts of ending my own life, a despair I was now openly discussing with my psychiatrist.

Isaac's birth had unconsciously revived memories of my past family, rekindling the pain and anguish I had worked so hard to bury. The fear of history repeating itself, of losing my newfound family, tormented me relentlessly. My anxiety intensified, and as I battled these ghosts of my past, I was struck by episodes of depression. Anxiety had me in a chokehold. It was like having a sense of dread or fearing the worst like the world was speeding up or slowing down at the same time. I felt like I could not stop worrying about my family or that bad things would happen if I stopped worrying. Isaac and Rachel became so precious to me that I could not imagine them getting harmed in any way.

I was so overprotective of Isaac and his well-being that it had started to disrupt my ability to focus on anything else, including my work. I knew I needed help, and it was with a sense of gratitude toward Rachel that I finally let go of my pride and sought assistance.

My psychiatrist, seeing the depth of my emotional struggles, recommended that I turn to the Veteran Administration (VA) for additional support. With a disability rating of 30% at that time, I began seeing another psychiatrist at the VA Hospital. It was during these sessions that a startling revelation came to light – I should have received psychiatric help much earlier, particularly after the incident in the Marine Corps. My therapist could not understand why I was not offered help at that exact moment.

My anxiety was only made worse by the horrific events of the Sandy Hook Elementary School shooting on December 14, 2012, in Newtown, Connecticut. At that time, Isaac was just in the second grade. Upon receiving the heartbreaking news while at work, I did something impulsive and deeply driven by my anxiety, fear, or trauma. Call it whatever you want, but it felt like the right thing to do as a father.

Without uttering a single word to anyone, I left my workplace and drove straight to Isaac's school. There, I remained seated in his classroom for the remainder of the day. My fears had led me to believe that there might be a copycat threat targeting Isaac's school, and I couldn't bear the thought of him being in danger. I wished that no parent would have to go through the traumatic events of school shootings because I knew the pain of losing a loved one.

This was but a glimpse into the overwhelming anxiety that gripped me when it came to my son. Managing my anxiety and depression was an ongoing journey, one that continued with regular sessions with my psychiatrist and participation in self-help groups.

As I left my job at Starcrest Products of California, where I had dedicated 15 years of my life, I found myself standing at a crossroads. Uncertainty loomed ahead because so many of my close friends and colleagues had left this mortal world, but my unwavering faith led me to seek God's guidance once more. My VA disability rating increased by another 10%, and with newfound hope, I received a letter stating that I might qualify for vocational rehabilitation.

This remarkable opportunity presented itself just a week after I bid farewell to my previous employment at Starcrest. I seized the chance and quickly applied for it. To my astonishment, I was approved to receive vocational rehabilitation support. The path forward became clear – I would enroll in our local community college.

Fortunately for me, the VA extended its support beyond tuition, covering the cost of my books, supplies, and even my cost of living while I attended college full-time. My mission for the next two years was straightforward: attend Moreno Valley Community College and pursue my education.

I did not mind being the "old man" on campus. I embraced it and dedicated myself to my studies. In June of 2015, I proudly received my Associate of Arts in Social and Behavioral Studies, achieving this milestone with distinction. However, I wasn't content to leave it at that.

With firm determination, I petitioned the VA for an extension to pursue my Bachelor's Degree, and lo and behold, they graciously approved my request. This led me to California Baptist University (CBU), where I embarked on the next phase of my academic journey.

For the next year and a half, I again dedicated myself to my studies at CBU, which concluded with receiving my Bachelor of Science in Organizational Leadership degree as I graduated "Cum Laude" in December 2016. It was proof of the power of faith in God.

It was amazing what had happened when I stepped out on faith and faith alone; God took over. As I prepared for my graduation, I set my sights on a new professional chapter. I applied for a position at Amazon, leveraging my newfound qualifications. Little did I know that the interview process at Amazon would prove to be unlike any other I had experienced.

I underwent three intensive phone interviews, each conducted by different Operation Managers. They had called me and asked if I had a pencil and paper at the ready before launching into complex production questions, challenging me with different scenarios and giving me a mere five minutes to formulate responses. These assessments aimed to gauge my problem-solving skills and my ability to enhance production metrics, such as "units per manhour" (UPM). They had even asked me how I would move people around to improve production and make the unit per manhour goal.

Following these phone interviews, I received an invitation for an in-person interview, a difficult eight-hour test that involved conversations with five additional Operation Managers. The interview included a written test administered on-site. It was a hard evaluation process, and I couldn't help but notice that I was the oldest candidate that day, surrounded by recent, young-looking college graduates, many with engineering degrees.

However, fate smiled upon me, and in January 2016, mere weeks after graduating from CBU, I received the news that I had been waiting for. Amazon offered me a position as an Area Manager at the "Ont 6" Distribution Center, overseeing the Amazon Fulfillment Engine (AFE), otherwise known as the packing area.

Although I had managed large groups of people before, it was nothing like what was going on at Amazon. I had over a hundred people that I was responsible for, but they were working on different shifts. How was I supposed to manage people that I could not even see in person? The only thing I could analyze was their productivity.

In my pursuit of effective management, I took it upon myself to meet every employee, a commitment that set me apart. In my first month, I didn't limit myself to just my assigned shift; I ventured into others, introducing myself individually to each team member.

It was a unique approach, perhaps even unprecedented in Amazon's history because I was the only manager who took the initiative to meet each and every individual working under me. The stress of my new role was evident; once that conveyor belt started rolling, every employee had to be in their designated stations, or I had to have a backup; otherwise, we wouldn't make our "units per manhour (UPM)" targets. If the UPM targets weren't met, we'd receive emails from Operations Managers and even Seattle, demanding explanations for the shortfalls and asking for concrete plans to rectify them, such as, "Why did you not make your UPM and what are you currently doing to make your UPM for the next hour?" This relentless pace extended over ten exhausting hours each day.

After our shifts, we would convene with Operations Managers to dissect the day's challenges, drafting strategies to overcome barriers for the following day. This meant that what had started as a ten-hour day routinely stretched into twelve or thirteen hours of relentless effort.

There was an unexpected silver lining to this intense environment. My physical health improved dramatically; I shed 35 pounds within the first 90 days. However, the strain on my knees, ankles, and back began to take its toll, leaving me in agony.

Despite the promising career path that Amazon offered, my pursuit of a "work-life balance" became increasingly dominant. Regrettably, my tenure at Amazon was short-lived, less than a year, cut short by my body's inability to keep up with the demands of the role. If I was younger, like the rest of the Managers, I would have never left.

So, I shifted gears once more and set my sights on the County of Riverside. I applied for a position as a Procurement Contract Specialist, yearning to return to my passion for procurement. The hard and tough interview process included meetings with multiple individuals, including a panel of six managers and the County Purchasing Manager, Mark Whitesell.

To my delight, I was offered the position, with my official start date falling on November 24, 2016. It was an unusual start date, to say the least – Thanksgiving Day. That's right, my first day with the County was a holiday. As I started on this new professional journey, Mark informed me that I would be assigned to the Sheriff's Department, making me the first Procurement Contract Specialist (PCS) to serve this department.

I appreciated the opportunity to work under Mark's leadership. His management style closely mirrored that of Mark Gray, a style that resonated with me. However, I soon learned that my enthusiasm for the Sheriff's Department wasn't shared by my fellow PCSs. None of them wanted to be assigned to the Sheriff's Department, a detail that puzzled me. I was the only one excited to be assigned to the Sheriff's Department and couldn't wait to move over to the department and start working.

I was eager to dive into the challenges of this unique role. My very first Request for Proposal (RFP) involved the Maintenance Agreement for the County's five Correctional Facilities. It quickly became evident that the Correctional

Facilities were in dire condition, and the Deputies voiced their concerns about the inadequate maintenance.

During my initial meeting with the Deputies, I boldly declared, "That's what you get when you go with the lowest bidder." My comment was met with stunned silence. They all stared at me like I was crazy. I could tell that I had touched a nerve.

I asked, "Did I say something wrong?"

They explained that County Purchasing had always gone with the lowest bidder, and that is why they were in this current situation. I attempted to educate them on the weighted criteria used in the RFP process, emphasizing that cost wasn't always the primary factor. My message struggled to gain traction, and despite our efforts, the contract was awarded to a vendor other than the lowest bidder, leading to the termination of the existing vendor's contract.

This episode underscored a crucial lesson – selecting the lowest bidder doesn't always translate to the best value. What I found most satisfying was my ability to negotiate a $1.2 million cost reduction in my very first contract with the County of Riverside. The County Purchasing Director and Mark Whitesell, the County Purchasing Manager, were understandably curious about my negotiation techniques and asked me how I was able to get the new company to reduce their price.

I explained that in the private sector, I had always negotiated until the contract was inked. After all, every dollar spent was taxpayer money, right? And we had a responsibility to steward it wisely. It was a principle I intended to uphold in every contract negotiation, putting the taxpayers' interests first.

Another issue that caught my attention was the Sheriff's Department's longstanding practice of renting a trash container for over a decade. Without hesitation, I terminated the rental agreement and arranged for the purchase of a new container immediately. It took me over a year to earn the trust of the Sheriff's Department Executive Staff, only to have an election a year later, and a new Sheriff was elected, meaning a whole new Executive Staff that did not trust Purchasing.

With a new Sheriff came a fresh Executive Staff eager to make their mark. Unfortunately, their enthusiasm was accompanied by a lack of understanding of government procurement regulations. At times, they viewed County Purchasing as a bottleneck, and I found myself in the role of an educator, explaining the complex procurement process. My goal was clear – no one, including myself, would go to jail due to misunderstandings about procurement regulations.

Yet again, it took me a year of persistent effort to establish trust with the new Executive Staff. My tenure at the Sheriff's Department was a time of both challenge and fulfillment.

Over six years, we accomplished much, procuring critical assets such as a new Search and Rescue Helicopter and Mobile Command Centers, among many other contracts. However, there were disappointments along the way, notably our inability to secure a state-of-the-art Computer Aid Dispatch (CAD) system, despite our dedicated and hard efforts for it. I decided to leave that particular issue untouched, as the wound was still fresh.

In the twilight of my career with the County, I managed to achieve something which I'm immensely proud of. My final Request for Proposal (RFP) was for Body-Worn Cameras, a project that carried significant importance. Yes, the last contract that I sent to the Board of Supervisors for approval was a 10-year contract for state-of-the-art Axon 3 Body Worn Cameras that was approved.

People often asked me why I chose to leave the County, and multiple factors and different aspects influenced my decision. Chief among them was my health. Twelve years in the Marine Corps, two tours of Drill Instructor Duty, and my time as an Instructor at NCO Leadership School had taken a toll on my body. There were mornings when the simple act of getting out of bed proved agonizing.

It's worth noting that I haven't mentioned retirement. Retirement, as I saw it, wasn't a concept I believed in, and the word 'retirement' is not mentioned in the Bible. And as you'll soon discover in the next chapter, there's no such thing as retirement when faith and purpose continue to drive you forward.

College Graduation.

Chapter 24: A New Beginning

Rachel and I had always believed in attending a church within our own neighborhood. Therefore, when we moved to Riverside County, it was no different. We began our search for a local church, one close to our home, and we found a predominantly white Christian church. We both became active members, forming new friendships and engaging in the congregation's activities.

The Pastor at the time happened to be the founding Pastor and was a warm and pleasant man. We admired his style of presenting the Sunday messages. While the church had a small percentage of Black, Hispanic, and Asian members, they had been part of the congregation for a long time. What stood out most to us about the founding Pastor was how he guided the congregation when they became overly concerned about worldly politics or social issues that didn't directly pertain to their faith.

One instance that I particularly appreciated was when the California Gay Rights Bill was on the ballot, and the congregation was very agitated. So, the pastor addressed their concerns during one of his sermons.

He asked a profound question, "Whether the bill passes or fails, how would that affect your personal relationship with Jesus Christ?"

His words resonated deeply, and there was a pin-drop silence in the sanctuary. It was a reminder that we are all guilty of often worrying about things beyond our control; we allow them to be a distraction from our faith in God.

Even with everything going on in the world we live in today - earthquakes, floods, famine, wars, and rumors of wars - the Bible had already brought up all of these things as signs of the end times, so I asked myself, 'How is this affecting my personal relationship with Jesus Christ?'

As time went on, the founding pastor retired and relocated to be closer to his grandchildren. The church found a new lead pastor, a younger but equally promising individual, and his family moved to California to lead our congregation. It was evident that they were meant to be here. This new pastor and his family were made to lead this church.

Under the new pastor's leadership, the church saw a revitalization with a more diverse congregation. As the chief administrator retired, they had just hired a new music director and youth pastor. Our connection to the church deepened, especially when the new pastor encouraged more congregation members to get involved. He asked for volunteers to welcome others at the beginning of the service and to lead communion. He personally asked me to participate, and though hesitant at first, I eventually accepted the role. Speaking in front of the congregation was a challenge that ultimately helped me grow.

As time went by, I became very comfortable speaking in front of the congregation. I wanted to thank the lead pastor for challenging me to speak. Even after more than ten years of attending, Rachel and I would chuckle whenever other churchgoers would come up to us and say, "Welcome to our church." It felt like someone welcoming us into our own home.

I attempted to attend the Men's Bible Study, but it didn't sit well with me because it would veer into political discussions. However, I still participated in men's outings like the Men's Barbecue, and on one occasion, I was the guest speaker. I sometimes felt uncomfortable when some members would wear MAGA caps, but I chose to ignore it, not thinking much of it. I had no problem with people wearing MAGA caps. Where I disagreed with the MAGA movement was that no one person can make America Great. America is still the Greatest Country in the world. And it would remain that way until God chooses differently. God and only God raises and lowers nations, not man.

However, everything changed with the tragic murder of George Floyd in May of 2020. Rachel and I were feeling all kinds of emotions, including devastation, anger, and frustration. We were seeking comfort and sympathy from our church and its community. Strangely, no one spoke about the murder; it was as if it hadn't happened.

In my search for solace, I submitted a prayer request on the church website, asking for a prayer to end systemic racism. To my shock, someone removed my prayer request. Undeterred, I posted another prayer request, this time on the men's website, with the same intent to end systemic racism. Once again, someone took it down.

I was beyond frustrated and furious. So, I decided to call the lead pastor directly and inquire about the removal of my prayer requests. His response left me stunned. He claimed that he did not know anything about it and revealed that he had been removed from the church campus and instructed to take a six-month sabbatical. I was in total shock when he told me that. The disappointment and devastation in the tone of his voice were evident.

I began making calls to understand the situation better. What I heard, though not confirmed, was that the new music director and the youth minister were allegedly orchestrating a coup to remove the lead pastor and his family.

My immediate question after hearing this was, "Where are the elders?"

In my quest for more information regarding the removal of my prayer requests, I learned that they were, indeed, taken down by the music director, who stated that the church should not be involved in politics. This infuriated me even further, as they seemed to equate George Floyd's murder with politics.

At this point, I had had enough. I prayed to God, seeking His guidance. After much reflection, meditation, and prayer, I felt that after over 15 years of dedicated membership in this church, it was time for me to move on. However, I couldn't ask or impose this decision on Rachel, so we discussed it, and I told her what I had chosen to do. She cried, and together, we prayed.

In the end, she told me, "Where you go, I go."

Leaving the church was hard and painful for both of us, but I couldn't imagine attending a church that couldn't offer even a semblance of sympathy or empathy to a loyal church member in need. They never allowed the lead pastor to return despite the congregation growing significantly from 25% to 30% under his leadership. Eventually, he and his family moved back East.

As word got out to the church that I had no plans to return, I received a call from one of the elders. He reached out to me, asking me to reconsider. He also mentioned that they were considering making me an elder. I remember that I replied, "I thought elders were supposed to protect the lead pastor of the church."

I also wondered why they would offer me this role now after 15 years, and it puzzled me that they'd only extended this offer now. Nonetheless, I humbly declined the offer of potentially becoming the first Black elder in this church's history.

About a year later, I learned that both the music director and the youth director were no longer part of the church. Go figure!

This marked the first time Rachel and I weren't members of a church. We felt alone and confused. I turned to televised sermons, finding refuge in the words of Charles Stanley and Tony Evans. They were my favorites. Still, I yearned for a sense of connection. I also wanted to contribute/serve and tithe to a local church. So, I prayed for guidance in finding a new local church to attend. During that time, I remember seeing Bishop Sykes, lead Pastor for CrossWord Christian Church around the city, and I kept running into him at the local Best Buy and community events. He never once asked me to come to CrossWord, but he did ask if I had a place to worship, and I respected that. So, I decided to visit the CrossWord Christian Church website and research their beliefs about God, Jesus Christ, and the Holy Spirit. It was important to me that their teachings aligned with my understanding of the Bible. Once satisfied, I started watching their sermons on YouTube. I joined the church online that same month, and a leader of the Men's Group contacted me right away.

Shortly after that, a Deacon introduced me to an associate pastor, Pastor Coop, in charge of the men's group. He leads the men's groups, and they are called Iron Men. I began attending their online Bible study meetings every Saturday morning.

Over the course of the next two years, my connection to this church deepened. It was a place where I felt my faith growing stronger. Eventually, I was approached about becoming a deacon. After months of prayer and seeking guidance from God, I accepted the role earlier this year. It has been a rewarding and humbling experience.

Back when I worked at Starcrest Products of California, Cindy Whitaker, our HR, was killed by a juvenile who had stolen a car and was involved in a high-speed chase that led to the accident. To cope with the grief and anger, I decided to volunteer at our local Police Department as a Citizen Patrol. I knew I had to do something to help catch the person who killed Cindy.

Becoming a volunteer was a way for me to cope with losing a colleague and friend. I attended the Police Academy and became a Citizen Patrol Volunteer, dedicating nearly two years to this service. Eventually, they found the juvenile, and he was prosecuted; therefore, I stopped volunteering. It provided a different perspective on the police force and its role in our community. I encouraged others to consider volunteering with their local police departments to understand better the challenges and responsibilities officers face.

I really enjoyed volunteering, so I looked at other ways to volunteer. So, as my journey of volunteering continued, I joined the Semper Fi #1 Memorial Honor Detail at the Riverside National Cemetery. This role allowed me to honor veterans and their families by participating in memorial services. I volunteered with the Semper Fi #1 Memorial Honor Detail while working as the Procurement Contract Specialist at the Riverside County Sheriff's Department, which made it somewhat challenging. I volunteered there for over a year and a half.

During a job walk at one of the five correctional facilities in Riverside County, God put it in my heart to become a chaplain so I could serve in a greater capacity.

I contacted the Riverside County Sheriff's Chaplain and told him what God had put in my heart, to which he replied, "If God put it in your heart, who am I to stop you?"

So, I embarked on the path to becoming a chaplain. After filling out the application, undergoing a background check, and an interview, I was selected to attend the Chaplain Academy. I graduated from the Chaplain Academy on October 4, 2021, and was assigned as one of the chaplains at the Moreno Valley Police Department. On October 8, 2022, I became a member of the California Practical Chaplain Association.

Always remember that there is no concept of retirement in the Bible, and I firmly believe that. As long as one is breathing, they have a purpose. Finding your purpose and living it is a fulfilling endeavor. Helping others is one of life's greatest joys. I asked God to use me wherever He saw fit, and He led me to various opportunities to serve.

One example that stands out is when I used to walk downtown Riverside during my breaks. That is when my back and knees would allow me to walk. I often noticed a homeless man straining to read a book or newspaper during these walks.

I approached him one day and asked if he had glasses. He replied that someone had stolen his glasses. So, the next day, I went to a local drugstore and purchased a package of three reading glasses, along with some water and a muffin.

When I saw him again, I handed him the bag with the glasses, water, muffins, and some money and walked away without asking any questions.

The following day, I saw him wearing the glasses and reading a book without straining. It was a small act, but it was one way God used me to help another person. I believe that by asking God to use us, He will always find a way.

Life is a journey, and mine has been filled with challenges, change, and countless opportunities to grow, serve, and make a difference. As I look back on my path, I am reminded of Proverbs 3:5-6: "Trust in the Lord with all your heart and lean not on your own understanding; in all your ways submit to him, and he will make your paths straight."

These verses have guided me through my life's various ups and downs, and I look forward to continuing this journey with faith and purpose.

Chapter 25: For Those That Are Chosen and Not

"You didn't choose me. I chose you. I appointed you to go and produce lasting fruit so that the Father will give you whatever you ask for, using my name."

– John 15: 16

Divine Purpose and Choice: This verse emphasizes that believers are chosen by God for a specific purpose. It underscores the divine initiative in the relationship between humans and God. God appoints individuals to produce lasting, meaningful outcomes. The mention of asking in Jesus' name signifies the intimate connection believers have with God through Christ.

***

"Since God chose you to be the holy people he loves, you must clothe yourselves with tenderhearted mercy, kindness, humility, gentleness, and patience. Make allowance for each other's faults and forgive anyone who offends you. Remember, the LORD forgave you, so you must forgive others."

– **Colossians 3: 12 – 13**

Clothed in Mercy and Forgiveness: Colossians instructs believers to embody qualities such as mercy, kindness, humility, gentleness, and patience. It stresses the importance of forgiveness, emphasizing that just as the

Lord forgives, believers should also forgive others. This passage promotes compassion, understanding, and the practice of forgiveness in human relationships.

***

"Furthermore, because we are united with Christ, we have received an inheritance from God, or we have become God's inheritance. For He chose us in advance, and He made everything work out according to His plan."

— **Ephesians 1: 11**

God's Divine Plan and Inheritance: Ephesians speaks about believers being part of God's divine plan. It highlights the unity of Christ and the assurance that everything unfolds according to God's purpose. Believers are not only chosen but also part of God's inheritance. This verse conveys a sense of predestination and the fulfillment of God's overarching plan through believers' lives.

These Bible verses carry profound messages about divine guidance, love, forgiveness, and purpose.

These verses are interconnected through the themes of divine choice, purpose, love, forgiveness, and unity with God. In John 15:16, God's choice and purpose are evident. Colossians 3:12-13 elaborates on how believers, chosen by God, should reflect divine qualities like forgiveness and mercy in their interactions with others. Ephesians 1:11 reinforces the idea of being chosen and part of God's grand plan, emphasizing the importance of living a life in harmony with God's purpose.

Together, these verses underscore the divine relationship between God and believers. They emphasize not only God's selection of individuals but also the qualities believers should manifest, including forgiveness, compassion, and understanding. The connection lies in the unity of purpose, divine love, and the shared responsibility of reflecting God's attributes in human relationships.

***

A few weeks ago, an old friend responded to one of my posts on Facebook and stated, "Wish I had that relationship with God like you do, Ced."

This made me think about friends out there who may not have a relationship with God, and it prompted me to send this out.

I would like to share with you that you can have a relationship with God, just like I do. It all begins with believing and "having faith" in God's Word, which says:

"For God so loved the world that he gave His only Son, that whosoever believes in Him should not perish but have everlasting life."

– John 3:16

God's Love and Gift of Salvation: This verse from the Gospel of John encapsulates the essence of Christianity. It emphasizes God's immense love for humanity. God's love is so profound that He sacrificed His only Son, Jesus Christ, to offer salvation to the world. The verse conveys that whoever believes in Jesus will not face spiritual death but will attain eternal life. It underscores the universal nature of God's love and the inclusive invitation for all to experience everlasting life through faith in Jesus Christ.

"That if you confess with your mouth the Lord Jesus and believe in your heart that God raised him from the dead, you are saved."

— **Romans 10:9-10**

Confession, Belief, and Salvation: In these verses from the Book of Romans, the process of salvation is explained. It involves both confession and belief. Confessing with one's mouth that Jesus is Lord signifies a public declaration of faith, acknowledging Jesus' divine authority. Simultaneously, believing in the heart that God raised Jesus from the dead demonstrates a deep, personal faith in the resurrection, a cornerstone of Christian doctrine. According to these verses, this confession and belief lead to salvation, indicating a transformative relationship with God through Jesus Christ.

The connection between these verses lies in the fundamental Christian doctrine of salvation through faith in Jesus Christ. John 3:16 reveals the motivation behind salvation, which is God's boundless love for humanity. God's love is expressed through the sacrificial gift of His Son, Jesus, offering eternal life to all who believe in Him. Romans 10:9-10 elucidates the response required from individuals to receive this gift of salvation. Confessing Jesus as Lord and believing in His resurrection are essential components of faith that lead to salvation.

In essence, John 3:16 illustrates God's love and the universal offer of salvation, while Romans 10:9-10 outlines the individual's response to this offer. Together, these verses emphasize the foundational Christian belief that salvation is available to all through faith in Jesus Christ, facilitated by God's love and grace.

If you do believe in God's word, then you can express your faith in Him by praying the following prayer:

HEAVENLY FATHER, I believe that Jesus Christ is your Son and that He died on the cross to save me from my sins. I believe that He rose again to life and that He invites me to live forever with Him in heaven. Because of what Jesus has done, I ask you to forgive me of my sin and give me eternal life. Help me to live in a way that pleases and honors you. In Jesus' name, **Amen**.

If you decide to commit your life to Christ, your relationship with God has begun, and it is a journey. I recommend getting the New Believers Bible by Greg Laurie. Find a local Bible-believing church and stay connected.

Jesus replied, "You must love the Lord your God with all your heart, all your soul, and all your mind." This is the first and greatest commandment. A second is equally important: "Love your neighbor as yourself." The entire law and all the demands of the prophets are based on these two commandments."

- Matthew 22: 37–40

If you did not hear the calling and decided not to give your life to Christ, please know that you are loved, and you are still my brother and sister. I will never force my beliefs on you, and we all have a right to choose our own beliefs.

But I would like to offer some guidance from the Bible that I believe will change your life if you choose to read it. And it is found in the New Testament in Mathew Chapters 5, 6, and 7, "New Living Translation (NLT).

I leave this to everyone, regardless of your beliefs:

"If you really want to make an impact on someone's life, be extraordinarily generous, giving two things that you have an unlimited of, and cost you nothing; Kindness and Gratitude."

Rachel and I in Temecula CA 2023

Made in the USA
Columbia, SC
08 January 2024

30079797R00176